Understanding
World History

The Great Recession

Other titles in the series include:

Ancient Egypt
Ancient Greece
Ancient Rome
The Black Death
The Decade of the 2000s
The Digital Age
The Early Middle Ages
Elizabethan England
The History of Rock and Roll
The Holocaust
The Industrial Revolution
The Late Middle Ages
Pearl Harbor
The Renaissance
Victorian England

Understanding World History

The Great Recession

Stuart A. Kallen

Bruno Leone
Series Consultant

ReferencePoint Press®

San Diego, CA

© 2014 ReferencePoint Press, Inc.
Printed in the United States

For more information, contact:
ReferencePoint Press, Inc.
PO Box 27779
San Diego, CA 92198
www.ReferencePointPress.com

LIBRARY OF CONGRESS CATALOGING-IN-PUBLICATION DATA

Kallen, Stuart A., 1955-
  The Great Recession / by Stuart A. Kallen.
    pages cm. -- (Understanding world history)
  Includes bibliographical references and index.
  ISBN-13: 978-1-60152-596-3 (hardback)
  ISBN-10: 1-60152-596-6 (hardback)
1. Global Financial Crisis, 2008-2009--Juvenile literature. 2. Recessions--History--21st century--Juvenile literature. 3. Economic history--21st century--Juvenile literature. I. Title.
  HB37172008 .K35 2014
  330.9'0511--dc23
                                      2013001180

Contents

Foreword

When the Puritans first emigrated from England to America in 1630, they believed that their journey was blessed by a covenant between themselves and God. By the terms of that covenant they agreed to establish a community in the New World dedicated to what they believed was the true Christian faith. God, in turn, would reward their fidelity by making certain that they and their descendants would always experience his protection and enjoy material prosperity. Moreover, the Lord guaranteed that their land would be seen as a shining beacon—or in their words, a "city upon a hill,"—which the rest of the world would view with admiration and respect. By embracing this notion that God could and would shower his favor and special blessings upon them, the Puritans were adopting the providential philosophy of history—meaning that history is the unfolding of a plan established or guided by a higher intelligence.

The concept of intercession by a divine power is only one of many explanations of the driving forces of world history. Historians and philosophers alike have subscribed to numerous other ideas. For example, the ancient Greeks and Romans argued that history is cyclical. Nations and civilizations, according to these ancients of the Western world, rise and fall in unpredictable cycles; the only certainty is that these cycles will persist throughout an endless future. The German historian Oswald Spengler (1880–1936) echoed the ancients to some degree in his controversial study *The Decline of the West*. Spengler asserted that all civilizations inevitably pass through stages comparable to the life span of a person: childhood, youth, adulthood, old age, and, eventually, death. As the title of his work implies, Western civilization is currently entering its final stage.

Joining those who see purpose and direction in history are thinkers who completely reject the idea of meaning or certainty. Rather, they reason that since there are far too many random and unseen factors at work on the earth, historians would be unwise to endorse historical predictability of any type. Warfare (both nuclear and conventional), plagues, earthquakes, tsunamis, meteor showers, and other catastrophic world-changing events have loomed large throughout history and prehistory. In his essay "A Free Man's Worship," philosopher and mathematician Bertrand Russell (1872–1970) supported this argument, which many refer to as the nihilist or chaos theory of history. According to Russell, history follows no preordained path. Rather, the earth itself and all life on earth resulted from, as Russell describes it, an "accidental collocation of atoms." Based on this premise, he pessimistically concluded that all human achievement will eventually be "buried beneath the debris of a universe in ruins."

Whether history does or does not have an underlying purpose, historians, journalists, and countless others have nonetheless left behind a record of human activity tracing back nearly 6,000 years. From the dawn of the great ancient Near Eastern civilizations of Mesopotamia and Egypt to the modern economic and military behemoths China and the United States, humanity's deeds and misdeeds have been and continue to be monitored and recorded. The distinguished British scholar Arnold Toynbee (1889–1975), in his widely acclaimed twelve-volume work entitled *A Study of History,* studied twenty-one different civilizations that have passed through history's pages. He noted with certainty that others would follow.

In the final analysis, the academic and journalistic worlds mostly regard history as a record and explanation of past events. From a more practical perspective, history represents a sequence of building blocks—cultural, technological, military, and political—ready to be utilized and enhanced or maligned and perverted by the present. What that means is that all societies—whether advanced civilizations or preliterate tribal cultures—leave a legacy for succeeding generations to either embrace or disregard.

Recognizing the richness and fullness of history, the ReferencePoint Press Understanding World History series fosters an evaluation and interpretation of history and its influence on later generations. Each volume in the series approaches its subject chronologically and topically, with specific focus on nations, periods, or pivotal events. Primary and secondary source quotations are included, along with complete source notes and suggestions for further research.

Moreover, the series reflects the truism that the key to understanding the present frequently lies in the past. With that in mind, each series title concludes with a legacy chapter that highlights the bonds between past and present and, more important, demonstrates that world history is a continuum of peoples and ideas, sometimes hidden but there nonetheless, waiting to be discovered by those who choose to look.

Important Events of The Great Recession

2005
Home ownership in the United States reaches a historic level of 69 percent.

1994
President Bill Clinton announces the National Homeownership Strategy with the goal of increasing home ownership in low-income neighborhoods.

2001
The Federal Reserve drastically lowers interest rates from 6.5 percent to 1.75 percent to counter the short recession after the 9/11 terrorist attacks.

1990   **2000**

1999
The Financial Services Modernization Act is signed into law allowing banks and insurance companies to invest in stocks, mortgage-backed securities, and other financial products.

2006
In July, home prices peak in the United States, achieving their greatest average value before the housing bubble collapses.

2002
In July President George W. Bush sets a goal of increasing the number of minority homeowners to 5.5 million.

2003
Investor Warren Buffet calls credit default swaps "financial weapons of mass destruction."

2008

On September 15 the largest business failure in US history occurs when the financial firm Lehman Brothers files for bankruptcy; on September 16 the Federal Reserve announces it will rescue AIG with an $85 billion bailout; on October 3 Congress passes the Emergency Economic Stabilization Act, which sets aside $700 billion to purchase toxic mortgage assets from banks; in December Bush approves a $13.4 billion bailout of the auto industry.

2010

In May the European Union agrees to a $147 billion bailout of Greece; in July Congress passes the Dodd-Frank Wall Street Reform and Consumer Protection Act.

2012

On November 14, millions of demonstrators protest austerity measures in twenty-three European Union nations for the European Day of Action and Solidarity.

2010

2007

The Great Recession begins; Moody's and Standard & Poor's downgrade the triple-A ratings on hundreds of mortgage-backed securities, touching off a financial panic on Wall Street.

2011

On September 17 about one thousand protesters from the Occupy Wall Street movement gather for the first time in New York City's Zuccotti Park; on October 15 the Occupy movement inspires an international day of protest in 950 cities in eighty-two countries.

2013

Home prices jump more than 5 percent in twenty major US cities, the largest annual increase since the housing bubble popped in 2007.

2009

In January the United States loses over 740,000 jobs, the largest monthly decline in sixty years; in February Congress passes the American Recovery and Reinvestment Act, allocating $787 billion to stimulate the economy; in May Chrysler files for bankruptcy, followed by General Motors a month later; in June the Great Recession officially ends in the United States; on July 1, the Cash for Clunkers program sets off a car-buying frenzy as consumers take advantage of a $3,500–$4,500 federal rebate for old, inefficient vehicles.

The Defining Characteristics of the Great Recession

Billions of people throughout the world depend on the economy for their basic survival. People work and earn money to pay for food, housing, education, and medical care. Many also borrow money to pay for expensive items such as cars and houses. In addition, in the United States alone over 200 million people use credit cards to pay for countless consumer goods, from clothing to computers. Whether people are buying homes with loans, called mortgages, or using credit cards to buy groceries, lenders expect them to pay the money back along with a borrowing fee, called interest. If a bank gives too many loans to people who do not pay the money back, however, then it goes out of business, or fails.

Economic activity based on earning, spending, and borrowing money has created prosperity in the United States and other industrial nations for decades. There have also been several notable periods when economies slowed down, unemployment increased, and business profits fell. Between 1930 and the early 1940s, during a period known as the Great Depression, the world economy experienced a steep decline of historic proportions. By 1933 in the United States, over five thousand banks had failed, and 25 percent of all working-age adults were unemployed. Hundreds of thousands of Americans—unable to pay their mortgages—were homeless and forced to live with their families in cars, trucks, tents, and homemade shacks. Unemployment in some areas of the United Kingdom reached 70 percent, and similar economic problems ravaged Canada, Germany, France, Spain, and other nations.

Depression and Recession

The Great Depression was triggered by a rapid collapse of the US stock market on October 29, 1929. At the time, millions of Americans had invested their life savings in the stock market and were wiped out financially. After the crash, sales of clothes, cars, and other consumer goods slowed considerably, and countless businesses went bankrupt.

In the aftermath of the Depression, laws were passed in the United States and elsewhere that regulated the practices of banks and investment firms such as those on Wall Street. Although an economic disaster on the scale of the Great Depression has not recurred in the United States, other recessions have taken place. These are spans during which economic activity contracts and unemployment rises by more than 1.5 percent. One of the most notable recessions occurred between 1973 and 1975 when a spike in oil prices and a downturn in the stock market pushed unemployment above 9 percent.

Although recessions also occurred in the early 1980s and the early 1990s, none could be compared to the Great Depression. However, many thought another Great Depression was at hand when, in December 2007, the global economy slid into a steep financial decline. Because the period was not technically as bad as a depression, the slowdown of 2008–2009 was named the Great Recession. And even after the government said the recession had ended in June 2009, severe worldwide economic problems continued to trouble many people.

Banks and Bubbles

The causes of the Great Recession were extremely complex but had very real consequences. In the broadest sense, the Great Recession was triggered by banks and financial firms on Wall Street. In the years leading

Home foreclosure signs became a common sight in neighborhoods around the country during the Great Recession. Loose lending practices and job losses contributed to the sharp rise in the number of people who lost their homes.

up to the recession, banks—encouraged by the government—loosened their lending practices. They began giving mortgages to people who might not have qualified for home loans in the past.

As money became easier to obtain, home prices soared, unnaturally inflated by the easy money the banks were loaning. This created what is called a housing bubble. During this period, many people qualified for loans for which they normally would not have been eligible. By 2006 millions found they were unable to make their monthly mortgage payments, so they defaulted on, or stopped paying back, their loans. This resulted in foreclosure, a legal process by which the bank repossesses the house, evicts the residents, and attempts to recover its loss by reselling the property. By 2007 so many people had defaulted, and so many homes had been foreclosed upon, that there were more houses for sale than people to buy them. This caused a rapid decline in housing prices. As a result, people were left owing more on their mortgages than their homes were worth. Many simply walked away from their homes, leaving banks with about $800 billion in unpaid loans. The result was the collapse, or near collapse, of the some of the world's largest banks, including Citigroup, Bank of America, Wachovia, and Washington Mutual.

European financiers had invested billions in American banks. This allowed the economic problem in the United States to spread quickly to Europe, also gripped by a bursting housing bubble and bank failures. In the United States and Britain alone over one hundred major banks failed, and dozens more were threatened. The recession resulted in a massive decline in the stock market. In October 2008 alone, stock prices fell by more than 18 percent, a decline not seen since the Great Depression.

The recession quickly moved beyond Wall Street to affect small businesses and average families. In early 2009 foundering banks stopped lending not only for mortgages but for small businesses that depended on temporary loans, called lines of credit, to stay in business. Many of these businesses failed, causing many more people to become unemployed. Credit became nearly impossible to obtain. People had less money to spend, so they shopped less, bought fewer cars, put off home remodeling, and did not take vacations. Since consumer spending drives about 75 percent of the American economy, this caused problems for everyone from construction workers to clerks at shopping malls. The big three auto makers in Detroit were particularly hard hit. General Motors, Chrysler, and Ford faced imminent bankruptcy. The federal government stepped in to provide billions of taxpayer dollars to the auto industry in a massive bailout.

A Deep Wound

Despite measures taken by the government to help car companies and banks, millions lost their jobs during the Great Recession. By 2009 unemployment had climbed to nearly 10 percent in the United States, up from only 4 percent in 2005. Figures were much worse in Greece, Ireland, and Spain, where 25 percent of workers were unemployed. As German economist Hans-Werner Sinn explains, in 2008 and 2009, "The world financial system nearly collapsed, and only with gigantic rescue measures have governments been able to prevent the worst and stabilize the world. The crisis left a deep wound. It will take the world years to recover."[1]

While the Great Recession was technically over by 2010, the economic problems resulting from this event took a heavy toll on typical families. On average, Americans lost 40 percent of their net worth between 2007 and 2010, an amount equal to twenty years' worth of wealth accumulation. This was largely due to the collapse in the housing market, with the median value of an average American home falling by 42 percent between 2007 and 2010. Poverty in the United States rose from 12 percent in 2007 to over 15 percent in 2012, with higher rates in California and elsewhere.

According to a 2012 report by the organization Better Markets, the total cost of the recession in the United States was $12.8 trillion. And many more costs could not be measured in monetary terms. As Better Markets notes, these include "the human suffering that accompanies unemployment, foreclosure, homelessness and related damage."[2]

Chapter 1

What Conditions Led to the Great Recession?

I n the early 2000s buying and selling homes was an international craze. Television viewers in the United States could watch at least half a dozen shows with titles like *Flip That House* and *Flipping Out*. The shows featured people who bought houses and performed minor repairs. At the time, housing prices were rising so quickly that the houses could be sold for a higher price—or "flipped"—within a few months. Similar shows in the United Kingdom had titles such as *The Property Ladder* and *Homes Under the Hammer*. Television was not the only media catering to the house flipping fad. Publishers released dozens of books such as *Real Estate Flipping: Grow Rich Buying and Selling Property* and *Flipping Houses for Dummies*.

House-flipping books and television shows were of great interest to people like Angel Cooley, a former judge who moved to Las Vegas in 2002. Cooley flipped eight houses in three years. In 2005 she told *Money* magazine, "you could buy [a house] in Vegas for $200,000, and in less than four months you could gain $150,000. It was a crazy kind of hysteria here."[3]

Changes in Lending

The idea of turning quick profits in the housing market was nothing new; savvy real estate investors had been doing it for decades. However, in the 2000s several factors converged to draw countless people like Cooley into the house-flipping business. During the decade, government policies in the United States and elsewhere led to historically low interest rates, fees that banks charge for borrowing money. These are based on rates set by the Federal Reserve, the central bank of the United States.

In 2006 interest rates were around 5.5 percent, down from as much as 9 percent in 1995. The lower interest rates had positive benefits: they allowed businesses to borrow money and grow, which stimulated the economy. In the housing market, low interest rates made mortgage payments much more affordable. For example, the monthly payment on a $300,000 mortgage in 2005 was about $2,400 a month at 5.5 percent whereas it would have been $3,000 a decade earlier when interest rates were 9 percent. Whether a person was buying a house to flip within a year or to live in for ten years, the low interest rate provided an incentive to home buyers.

As the government was lowering interest rates, banks were loosening the rules for borrowing money. This meant banks were providing mortgages to people with low incomes or bad credit who might not have qualified for loans in earlier decades. These loans, which had higher interest rates, were very profitable for banks and fueled the housing bubble.

Even if home owners did not sell their houses, they could still take advantage of rising home prices. If someone owned a house and its value increased, so did the owner's equity, which is the difference between what is owed on the house and its market value. For example, if a house was bought for $300,000, and its value increased to $400,000, that owner then had $100,000 in equity. He or she could then apply for what is called a home equity loan, or a second mortgage, and borrow that $100,000 from a bank. However, if the loan was not repaid, the bank would take possession of the home.

Before the Great Recession began in 2007, home equity loans were extremely easy to obtain. People often used the money to remodel their homes, buy cars, or take expensive vacations.

Prime Rate Loans

The lending standards in the early 2000s were extremely loose compared to those in the previous decades. Before the 2000 housing boom,

Rapidly rising housing prices in the early 2000s heightened the appeal of house flipping. House flippers bought houses, made minor changes such as replacing kitchen cabinets, and then quickly sold them for a profit.

people who received mortgages had to prove they earned enough income to make monthly mortgage payments. To do so, prospective borrowers had to provide copies of tax forms and paychecks. Typically, the paperwork needed to show that the borrower earned three times more every month than the amount of the mortgage payment. As investment manager and journalist Nomi Prins explains, "The idea was that lenders wanted to protect the money they lent, and borrowers wanted to make sure they were good for that money."[4] In addition, anyone wanting a mortgage had to have a good credit history. Banks had to be satisfied that borrowers made timely payments on car loans, credit cards, and even utility bills.

In the second half of the twentieth century, the majority of home loans were known as prime rate mortgages. The prime rate was the interest rate banks charged their preferred customers who had good credit ratings. The majority of prime rate mortgages were thirty-year loans, which meant the borrower paid back the money over a period of 360 months. Prime rate mortgages had a fixed interest rate, which meant the interest rate never changed throughout the entire payback period.

To qualify for a prime rate mortgage, borrowers generally had to make a down payment from their own funds, equal to 20 percent of the purchase price of a home. This meant someone buying a $250,000 home was required to make a down payment of $50,000 to qualify for a $200,000 mortgage. The large down payment is what renowned investor Warren Buffet referred to as having "skin in the game."[5] Buffet meant that the buyer had a personal investment, or stake, in the transaction, which would ensure they would keep up with the monthly payments and presumably avoid foreclosure.

When borrowers qualified for a prime rate loan, they had to pay additional fees called closing costs that were incurred as part of the complicated real estate transactions. Closing is the point in time when a seller transfers property to the buyer. Closing costs include lawyer fees for preparing contracts, money paid to inspectors to make sure the property is in good condition, commissions paid to real estate agents, and taxes and filing fees charged by various government entities. Closing costs could be several thousand dollars. They were due, along with the down payment, at closing.

Throughout much of the twentieth century, the majority of prime rate mortgages were obtained through banks called savings and loans, or S&Ls. These banks had a simple business model. Customers deposited their savings in the bank. This money was loaned to people for mortgages and other needs. The bank made money from the interest on the loans. Bank workers serviced the loans; that is, they made sure the money was paid back in a timely manner. Bank officers at savings and loans were extremely careful about to whom they made loans. If too many loans were not paid back, the bank might fail.

Loosening Lending Standards

These stringent standards for mortgages meant that many people were disqualified from home ownership. However, in 1994 President Bill Clinton laid out a plan called the National Homeownership Strategy to rapidly increase home ownership among minorities. The complex plan included numerous actions that encouraged banks to loosen lending standards.

President Bill Clinton unveils his administration's National Homeownership Strategy in 1995. The program's goal was to create 8 million new US homeowners by the year 2000—especially in low-income communities.

Lenders were also encouraged to take low down payments in order to make home ownership easier for first-time buyers. In a speech, Clinton explained that the National Homeownership Strategy was needed because "more Americans should own their own homes, for reasons that are economic and tangible, and reasons that are emotional and intangible, but go to the heart of what it means to harbor, to nourish, to expand the American Dream."[6] One year after the National Homeownership Strategy was instituted home prices began to rise and continued to do so until 2005.

Clinton's successor, President George W. Bush, continued the government push to increase home ownership in low-income communities. In July 2002 Bush set a goal of increasing the number of minority home owners by 5.5 million, stating, "Part of economic security is owning your own home."[7]

Subprime Loans

These changes in government policy triggered an explosion in the number of banks willing to lend to those with lower credit ratings. However, there was a much greater chance that people with low incomes would default on their loans (not pay them back). To account for this fact, lenders did not offer low-income applicants prime rate mortgages like those given by the old savings and loans. Instead lenders offered what were called subprime mortgages. These had interest rates that could be twice as high as those on prime rate loans. Subprime lenders also charged much more for closing costs. For example, in 2000 closing costs on a $300,000 prime rate loan were $5,000, while those on a similar subprime loan were $15,000.

In order to attract customers to loans with high interest rates and steep closing costs, subprime lenders pioneered a number of marketing techniques. By the early 2000s subprime lenders were offering mortgages with little or no money down. This meant a person could borrow several hundred thousand dollars without any up-front investment. Furthermore, closing costs, while high, were added to the initial loan and paid off over time with the monthly payments.

Rather than offering fixed interest rates, subprime lenders offered

For more than sixty-five years a Depression-era law called the Glass-Steagall Act prevented banks from buying and selling stocks. However, in 1999 Secretary of the Treasury Robert Rubin and President Bill Clinton worked with Republicans led by Senator Phil Gramm to repeal Glass-Steagall. Wall Street bankers, like Sanford Weill, the powerful CEO of Citigroup, lobbied for years for the repeal. The big banks wanted to invest their funds in the stock market and create new financial products such as mortgage-backed securities.

Glass-Steagall was replaced by the Financial Services Modernization Act of 1999. The new law allowed banks to invest their funds in the stock markets and deal in financial products such as mortgage-backed securities. Many people, including Weill, later came to believe that the financial panic of 2008 would never have ensued if the Glass-Steagall Act had remained in place. In 2012 Weill told CNBC that new laws based on Glass-Steagall needed to be enacted: "What we should probably do is go and split up investment banking from banking, have banks be deposit takers, have banks make commercial loans and real-estate loans, have banks do something that's not going to risk the taxpayer dollars, that's not too big to fail." However, Gramm still stands by the Financial Services Modernization Act, stating he didn't see "any evidence" that rolling back Glass-Steagall legislation "had anything to do with the financial crisis."

Quoted in *Huffington Post*, "Phil Gramm: Glass-Steagall Repeal Didn't Have 'Anything to Do with the Financial Crisis,'" July 26, 2012. www.huffingtonpost.com.

adjustable rate mortgages. The interest rates on these mortgages were adjusted, usually upward, over time, depending on complex calculations made by the lender and the Federal Reserve.

By 2003 most adjustable rate mortgages featured extremely low temporary interest rates. These were called "teaser rates" because they were meant to persuade or coax borrowers to apply for a subprime mortgage. In 2005, 40 percent of the mortgages written by Washington Mutual, or WaMu, offered a teaser rate of 1 percent. Other teaser rates might be anywhere from 2 to 4 percent.

What teaser rates all had in common was that they expired, or reset, after a time period lasting from four months to three years. When the interest rate reset it often jumped to a much higher level, up to 12 percent. This meant that the monthly mortgage payment on a $300,000 house with a 2 percent teaser rate would initially be about $1,000. If the loan was adjusted up to 12 percent when the teaser rate expired, the monthly payment would more than triple to $3,085.

Adjustable rate mortgages carried a high risk that the borrower would default on the loan when the monthly payment jumped. However, those who flipped homes planned to sell the property before the teaser rate ended. As James Theckston, regional vice president for Chase Home Finance in southern Florida, explains, "You've got somebody making $20,000 buying a $500,000 home, thinking that she'd flip it. That was crazy, but the banks put programs together to make those kinds of loans."[8]

Others with adjustable rate mortgages believed that they could refinance with a fixed rate loan when the teaser rate expired. The lenders encouraged this belief because they profited from closing costs and other fees during refinancing. Whatever the case, by 2005, 75 percent of all subprime mortgages came with adjustable rates. And that year home ownership in the United States climbed to historic levels with over 69 percent of adults living in homes they owned.

No-Document Loans

Many subprime lenders did not require prospective borrowers to provide extensive income documents, or "docs." These loans were called low-doc or no-doc loans, and they made it easy for loan applicants to exaggerate or lie about their income. Financial law professors Kathleen Engel and Patricia A. McCoy explain these loans:

[In] low-documentation loans, applicants reported their income, but did not provide proof. In a no-documentation loan, the loan was underwritten [guaranteed] with no information at all on the loan applicant's income. . . . Low-doc and no-doc loans were particularly noxious because they invited deep deception. They soon became known as "liar's loans." Borrowers could put whatever figure they wanted down for their income and not back it up with tax returns or pay stubs.[9]

With home prices climbing and banks eager to make loans, it is not surprising that people with little or no income wanted to buy homes. As investor Michael Burry states: "The borrowers will always be willing to take a great deal for themselves. It's up to the lenders to show restraint, and when they lose it, watch out."[10] However, lenders were showing little restraint because subprime loans were very profitable in the early 2000s.

"Less Savvy Borrowers"

Subprime loans originated with mortgage brokers, salespeople who sought out new customers for loans. Many brokers worked for large companies such as Countrywide Financial, which financed 20 percent of all subprime mortgages in the United States in 2006. According to Engel and McCoy, mortgage brokers often marketed subprime loans to "people who had been turned down for credit in the past because of discrimination or bad credit or both. . . . Subprime lenders plied racially mixed neighborhoods with credit, posting ads on telephone poles and billboards. Mortgage brokers, the foot soldiers of the subprime industry, hawked . . . loans door-to-door."[11]

Brokers were paid a commission for each buyer they signed, which meant the more mortgages they wrote, the more money they made. In addition, the commissions were much higher on risky loans because those were more profitable for the lender. According to Theckston, mortgage brokers "earned a commission seven times higher from subprime loans, rather than prime mortgages. So they looked for less savvy borrowers—those with less education, without previous mortgage experience, or without fluent English—and nudged them toward subprime loans."[12]

Mortgage-Backed Securities

Subprime lending institutions did not follow the old savings and loan business model based on lending their own money and servicing the mortgages for many years. Instead, subprime lenders grouped all their loans together into a large pool of debt. This pool was then divided up into financial instruments called mortgage-backed securities, which were sold like stocks and bonds. Investors who bought mortgage-backed securities collected the interest paid on the mortgages by home owners.

Creating mortgage-backed securities is called securitization. This allowed subprime lenders to earn a quick profit on long-term debt they incurred by writing thirty-year mortgages. Investigative reporter Matt Taibbi offers an explanation of this complicated financial operation:

> Say you make a hundred thirty-year loans to a hundred different homeowners, for $50 million worth of houses. Prior to securitization, you couldn't turn those hundred mortgages into instant money; your only access to the funds was to collect one hundred different meager payments every month for thirty years. But now the banks could take all one hundred of those loans, toss them into a pool, and sell the future revenue streams to another party for a big lump sum—instead of making $3 million over thirty years, maybe you make $1.8 million up front, today. And just like that, a traditionally long-term business is turned into a hunt for short-term cash.[13]

Four large Wall Street investment banks, Bear Stearns, Lehman Brothers, Goldman Sachs, and Citigroup, were the main institutions that turned pools of mortgages into mortgage-backed securities. These companies generated large fees from the securitization process and relied on a constant flow of loans from companies like Countrywide, WaMu, and others.

Betting on Securities

Mortgage-backed securities are financial instruments sold to investors. They are created from pools of mortgages. *Slate* contributor Chris Wilson explains why these securities could be good investments or bad:

> When the housing market is doing well and interest rates are low, investing in a mortgage-backed security is a fairly safe bet. So long as homeowners stay current with their payments, holders of mortgage-backed securities receive a stream of payments. Even those investors who buy lower-quality mortgage-backed securities, in the hopes of receiving higher interest payments, generally fare well in a bull [or rising stock] market. But when the housing market goes south, or if interest rates rise, even the safest of these investments are in serious jeopardy. Rising interest rates reduce the value of securities that pay a fixed rate of interest. When borrowers default on mortgages, the stream of payments available to holders of mortgage-backed securities declines. And when [an investor] has borrowed heavily to finance the purchase and trading of such securities, it doesn't take much of a fall in value to trigger serious problems. The nationwide mortgage-default crisis [of 2007–2008] harshly punished many of the participants in the mortgage-backed-securities market.

Chris Wilson, "What Is a Mortgage-Backed Security?," *Slate*, March 17, 2008. www.slate.com.

Three Levels of Risk

Creating mortgage-backed securities is a byzantine process that involves another entity called a bond rating agency. The two main Wall Street rating agencies in the early 2000s were Moody's Investors Service and Standard & Poor's (S&P). These companies used complex mathematical formulas to rate the value of each mortgage-backed security offered for sale to investors. After evaluating the securities, the agencies gave them grades, which depended on the relative investment risk. The top level security was rated AAA, or "Senior," which technically means "credit risk almost zero."[14] The middle level was BBB or "Mezzanine," and the lowest level was CCC or "Equity." Taibbi offers an example to clarify the ratings:

> Imagine a box with one hundred home loans in it. Every month, those one hundred homeowners make payments into that box. Let's say the total amount of money that's supposed to come in every month is $320,000. What banks did is split the box up into three levels and sell shares in those levels . . . [investors] who bought the AAA-level piece of the box were always first in line to get paid. The bank might say, for instance, that the first $200,000 that flowed into the box every month would go to the AAA investors. If more than $200,000 came in every month, in other words if most of the homeowners did not default and made their payments, then you could send the next payments to the B or "mezzanine" level investors—say, all the money between $200,000 and $260,000 that comes into the box. These investors made a higher rate of return than the AAA investors, but they also had more risk of not getting paid at all.[15]

Investors in the lowest CCC level received a return only if everyone in the pool paid their mortgage on time. While these securities at this level were risky, they cost less and the profits were greater.

One of the biggest banks in the world, Deutsche Bank in Germany, bought large quantities of CCC rated securities. While the institution's

Countrywide Financial financed 20 percent of all subprime mortgages in the United States in 2006. Lenders such as Countrywide initially profited from these risky loans thanks to extremely high interest rates and closing costs.

investors were aware of the risk, they bet that even those with bad credit could make their mortgage payments on time for a few years. According to Taibbi, "Their strategy was simple: buy the [CCC securities], cash in on the large returns for a while, and hope the homeowners in your part of the deal can keep making their . . . payments just long enough that the [bank] can eventually unload their loans on someone else before they start defaulting."[16]

The End of the Housing Bubble

Between 2002 and 2007 Moody's and Standard & Poor's earned record profits totaling $6 billion. Much of this money was paid by investment banks that expected Moody's and S&P to provide reliable ratings for mortgage-backed securities. This conflict of interest was described in a 2011 Senate report, *Wall Street and the Financial Crisis*:

> Credit rating agencies were paid by the Wall Street firms that sought their ratings and profited from the financial products being rated. . . . The ratings firms were dependent upon those Wall Street firms to bring them business and were vulnerable to threats that the firms would take their business elsewhere if they did not get the ratings they wanted. The ratings agencies weakened their standards as each competed to provide the most favorable ratings to win business and market share.[17]

Until the financial crisis, the interaction between rating agencies and Wall Street firms remained unknown to the general public. Most investors operated on the belief that buying AAA securities was close to risk-free. And between 2002 and 2007 seemingly risk-free securities were abundantly available. During that five-year period, ratings agencies gave AAA ratings to $3.2 trillion worth of mortgage-backed securities pooled from home buyers with bad credit or undocumented incomes. Without those AAA ratings, investors such as banks, insurance companies, pension funds, and private citizens would likely not have bought the securities.

The business of selling highly rated mortgage-backed securities faltered in late 2006 when the growing number of foreclosures began to make headlines. Many of the borrowers who faced foreclosure had come to the end of their two-year teaser rates and saw their monthly mortgage payments jump. At the same time the Federal Reserve raised interest rates, which made refinancing difficult.

By February 2007 home owners with subprime loans were defaulting in record numbers. Analyzing the trends, the nonpartisan home owners organization Center for Responsible Lending forecast that 2.2 million borrowers would lose their homes by the end of the year. This represented one in five subprime mortgages issued between 2005 and

2006. In 2007, as foreclosures increased, home prices began a downward trend. This led investors to stop buying mortgage-backed securities, which, in turn, dried up the flow of money to subprime lenders.

While other economic events were associated with the Great Recession of 2008, the major cause may be traced to the subprime loan business. Millions of Americans were enticed into buying homes with risky loans they could not afford. Subprime lenders earned huge profits for a time. Powerful Wall Street investment banks made billions of dollars selling AAA-rated mortgage-backed securities to investors throughout the world. Even before the Great Recession began, millions of people, from carpenters and brick layers to real estate agents and auto workers, suffered when the subprime lending business began to fail. Only after the housing bubble popped, and the surge nearly sank the economy, did people come to understand that their ability to earn a living was tied to complex and unsustainable deals made by the biggest players on Wall Street.

Chapter 2

Meltdown on Wall Street

"Wall Street" is the nickname for the financial district in New York City. It is home to the world's largest banks, stock brokerage firms, insurance companies, and the New York Stock Exchange (NYSE). On the stock exchange, the financial health of the US economy is measured by the ups and downs of the Dow Jones Industrial Average. This index tracks the stock prices of thirty major American companies such as ExxonMobil, Bank of America, Microsoft, and IBM. Rising stock prices are interpreted to mean that investors are showing confidence in the economy. Declining stock prices are a sign that the economy is weakening. When stock prices plunge, it indicates that economic hardships are ahead.

Some of the largest historic drops of the Dow Jones Industrial Average occurred between September and December 2008. And it was a small number of banks, brokers, and insurance firms located on Wall Street that sent the Dow tumbling and spread financial panic across the globe.

"The Monster That Ate Wall Street"

The Wall Street meltdown was triggered by the plunging value of mortgage-backed securities, which were bundles of subprime mortgages. These securities carried a special kind of insurance called a credit default swap (CDS). Despite the name, a CDS is not a swap. It is similar to an insurance contract that covers a loan from a bank. In case the loan is not paid back, the CDS covers the bank's loss. Between the late 1990s and 2007 billions of dollars worth of CDSs were sold by the huge insurance and financial services company American International Group (AIG) and other companies to cover losses on mortgage-backed securities.

In 2007 mortgage-backed securities lost their value when the housing bubble popped. The firms that sold CDSs were committed to paying for the losses. However, these firms did not have the hundreds of billions of dollars needed to pay them off. This left them teetering on the edge of bankruptcy. For this reason CDSs are referred to by financial journalist Matthew Philips as "the monster that ate Wall Street."[18]

"Win-Win"

The CDS "monster" was first devised in 1994 by the multinational investment bank JPMorgan, now called JPMorgan Chase. Bankers at JPMorgan were looking for ways to insure billions of dollars in

The financial health of the US economy is measured by the ups and downs of stock prices on the New York Stock Exchange (pictured). Historic drops in stock prices in late 2008 spread financial panic across the globe.

corporate bonds. Corporate bonds are issued by a company wishing to raise money to expand its business. For example, IBM might sell $10 million in bonds to expand one of its research facilities. If JPMorgan bought those bonds, it would essentially be loaning IBM $10 million. In return, JPMorgan would receive regular interest payments over the life of the bond, which might be five or ten years. When that period ended, the bond matured and the issuer, in this case IBM, would pay back the entire $10 million.

While the chance that IBM would go out of business was small, it was still a possibility. To lessen the risk that the bonds might not be paid off, JPMorgan invented CDSs. These were sold to a third party, usually another bank, an insurance company, or an investment company called a hedge fund. Whoever bought the swaps would pay IBM's debt to JPMorgan if IBM defaulted. The company that sold the swaps would benefit because JPMorgan would pay them monthly premiums, like those paid on a car insurance policy. If IBM did not default, the owners of the CDSs profited from the premiums they received over the years from JPMorgan. Matt Taibbi explains how this works:

> Say Bank A is holding $10 million in . . . IBM bonds. It goes to Bank B and makes a deal: we'll pay you $50,000 a year for five years and in exchange, you agree to pay us $10 million if IBM defaults sometime in the next five years—which of course it won't, since IBM never defaults. . . . It's a win-win. Bank B makes, basically, a free $250,000. Bank A, meanwhile, gets to lend out another few million more dollars, since its $10 million in IBM bonds is [now insured].[19]

Buying and Selling

Because of the perceived win-win nature, CDSs proved to be incredibly popular. In the mid-nineties JPMorgan created a CDS division and filled it with young math and science graduates from the best colleges in the United States and England. Before long other banks began selling CDSs, and the CDS market expanded rapidly. In 2000, $100 billion

Wall Street and the Financial Crisis

I n April 2011 Senators Carl Levin and Tom Coburn issued a Senate Permanent Subcommittee on Investigations report titled *Wall Street and the Financial Crisis*. In the following excerpt, the report explains the role the rating agencies Moody's and S&P played in triggering the Great Recession:

> This Report concludes . . . that the most immediate trigger to the financial crisis was the July 2007 decision by Moody's and S&P to downgrade hundreds of [mortgage-backed] securities. The firms took this action because, in the words of one S&P senior analyst, the investment grade [AAA] ratings could not "hold." By acknowledging that securities containing high risk, poor quality mortgages were not safe investments and were going to incur losses, the credit rating agencies admitted the emperor had no clothes. Investors stopped buying . . . and financial institutions around the world were suddenly left with unmarketable securities whose value was plummeting.

Carl Levin and Tom Coburn, *Wall Street and the Financial Crisis: Anatomy of a Financial Collapse,* US Senate Permanent Subcommittee on Investigations, April 13, 2011. www.hsgac.senate.gov.

worth of CDSs were issued. By 2004 that number had jumped to an estimated $6 trillion. The explosive growth was fueled by the fact that CDSs were more profitable than traditional investing. Business journalist Adam Davidson explains using General Electric (GE) as an example:

> Let's say you think GE is rock solid, that it will never default on a bond, since it hasn't in recent memory. You could buy a GE

bond and make, say, a meager 6 percent interest. Or you could just sell GE credit default swaps. You get money from other banks, and all you have to give is the promise to pay if something bad happens. That's zero money down and a profit limited only by how many [CDSs] you can sell. . . . Banks and hedge funds found that it was much easier and quicker to just buy and sell CDS contracts rather than buy and sell actual bonds. [20]

In this booming market, CDSs were not just sold to cover corporate bonds as JPMorgan originally intended. By the early 2000s the majority of CDSs were being sold to investors to protect mortgage-backed securities. This meant that trillions of dollars of mortgage debt was insured by institutions that were betting that the mortgage loans would be repaid.

"Potentially Lethal"

Despite the booming market, flaws with CDSs were seemingly ignored on Wall Street. Although a CDS was perceived as insurance, it was not like a car insurance policy. If a person wrecks a car, the insurance company is required by law to have money in its accounts to pay the policyholder for a new car. Institutions that bought CDSs were not required by law to have money, called collateral, on hand to pay off the swap. This led to large-scale problems because by 2007 the value of CDSs sold on Wall Street had reached $62 trillion. That shocking number was more than four times the gross national product (GNP) of the United States that year. (The GNP is the market value of all goods and services produced annually in a given country.) That number was also more than the GNP of the entire world, which was about $55 trillion at the time.

Despite their shortcomings, CDSs were endorsed by government banking regulators. Alan Greenspan, chairman of the Federal Reserve between 1987 and 2006, often stated that markets would regulate themselves without interference from the government. If a particular product, such as a CDS, was a bad deal, then banks and investors would not buy it. Greenspan believed that the risk of a financial crisis caused by

CDSs was "extremely remote," as he told a congressional banking committee in 2003: "What we have found over the years in the marketplace is that [CDSs] have been an extraordinarily useful vehicle to transfer risk from those who shouldn't be taking it to those who are willing to and are capable of doing so. It would be a mistake to increase regulation.[21]

While most investors put great stock in Greenspan's words, not everyone agreed. In 2003 Warren Buffet warned that CDSs were "financial weapons of mass destruction, carrying dangers that . . . are potentially lethal."[22]

A Triple-A Institution

Of all the companies on Wall Street, the insurance giant AIG was the most eager to assume the risks associated with CDSs. The company, founded in 1919, had been providing insurance to large corporations and major industries since 1962. By 2000 AIG operated insurance companies, retirement funds, and financial service divisions. AIG was the eighteenth largest company in the world, and it insured and advised more than 100,000 companies in 130 countries. The company had $40 billion cash on hand and gross sales of over $1 trillion a year.

One of the major parts of AIG was called the Financial Products division, or AIG FP. Financial Products developed complex, interlocking deals for numerous institutions around the world. Joseph Cassano, the head of AIG FP, describes the company's clients: "It's a broad global swath of mostly high-grade institutions, mostly high-grade entities around the world and it includes banks and investment banks, pension funds, endowments, foundations, insurance companies, hedge funds, money managers, high-net-worth individuals, municipalities and sovereigns [royals]."[23] AIG offered these private, government, and corporate entities deals to boost cash reserves, pay down debt, and guard against rising interest rates.

AIG was a highly esteemed company that earned a triple-A (or AAA) credit rating from Standard & Poor's. A corporation with a triple-A credit rating is considered extremely safe for lenders to invest their money in. According to Robert O'Harrow Jr. and Brady Dennis,

Car insurers are required by law to have money available to pay for repairing or replacing a policyholder's car after a wreck. Credit default swaps were wrongly viewed as similar to car insurance.

reporters at the *Washington Post*, it was "a Triple A institution as unlikely to default as the U.S. Treasury itself."[24]

As one of the largest insurance companies in the world, AIG, not surprisingly, would take part in the CDS business. In 2001 AIG Financial Products generated a $300 million profit from premiums on CDS contracts. The vast majority of these contracts were on relatively safe corporate bonds. However, in the years that followed, AIG invested heavily in CDSs based on mortgage-backed securities. By 2005 the company was committed to insuring $80 billion worth of mortgage-backed securities.

Eugene Park, one of the executives at Financial Products, began to question the wisdom of this business move. Park was worried that the housing market could crash in any part of the country at any time. He warned Cassano that AIG was too heavily invested in CDSs. The company soon stopped issuing swaps, but it was too late. Because of

AIG FP's massive investment in CDSs, Standard & Poor's downgraded AIG's credit rating from AAA to AA. When a company's credit rating is lowered, it has far-reaching consequences. In this case, AIG was required by law to put aside $450 million in collateral. This was proof it could pay off a percentage of its CDSs.

"Toxic" Assets

AIG's problems were magnified by a slowing real estate market. Then on July 10, 2007, a major shock wave shook Wall Street. Moody's announced that the default rate on subprime loans was much higher than previous expected. As a result, Moody's downgraded the AAA ratings on four hundred mortgage-backed securities. These securities were reclassified with the lowest CCC rating. Angelo Mozilo, the CEO of Countrywide, began referring to the CCC securities as "toxic"[25] assets, and the term was widely adopted by financiers, government officials, and the general public.

The same day Moody's made its announcement, S&P said it would cut the ratings on $12 billion worth of mortgage-backed securities. A month later Moody's downgraded another 690 mortgage-backed securities because of "dramatically poor overall performance."[26] The downgraded securities immediately lost three-quarters of their value. In the months that followed, the downgrading continued, and by early 2008 the ratings agencies had reclassified 90 percent of all mortgage-backed securities to CCC. This reduced their collective value by an astonishing $1.9 trillion.

"The Financial Crisis Was On"

Large investors such as pension funds were prohibited from owning low-rated securities and tried to sell the ones they held. This mass sell-off created a panic. In the months that followed, the Dow Jones Industrial Average continually headed downward. Meanwhile hundreds of companies that were invested in mortgage-backed securities and subprime loans declared bankruptcy, including Bear Stearns and

Countrywide Financial. As the *Wall Street and the Financial Crisis* Senate report notes, "The financial crisis was on."[27]

During this period most of AIG's CDSs were insuring securities owned by Goldman Sachs. In October Goldman demanded that AIG post collateral for $3 billion worth of CDSs on toxic assets. Instead, AIG posted $1.5 billion. After doing so, the price of AIG stock quickly dropped 25 percent. In November 2008 AIG's problems continued to grow. The company reported losses of $352 million on CDSs. That number would grow to $11.5 billion by February 2009.

By then economists had determined that the GNP of the United States had shrunk for the last two quarters of 2007 (a quarter equals three months). Unemployment had increased more than 1.5 percent. In economic terms, this activity meant that the United States had officially entered a recession. During this period home values tumbled in twenty-three of the twenty-five major metropolitan areas in the United States, as a record number of foreclosures pushed prices down.

"The World Is About to End"

As troubles continued with the subprime mortgage market, they caused great damage at one of Wall Street's oldest investment firms. Lehman Brothers—founded in 1850—was heavily invested in mortgage-backed securities, which were rapidly losing their value. In early September 2008 Lehman announced it had suffered a $3.9 billion loss in the previous three months. This sent the company's stock price plunging by 77 percent in one week.

On Friday, September 12, Secretary of the Treasury Henry Paulson decided that the government would not rescue Lehman Brothers with a financial bailout. Without intervention from the Treasury Department, the respected Wall Street firm was forced into bankruptcy. This stoked fears on Wall Street that the entire economy was about to collapse. When New York mayor Michael Bloomberg heard about Lehman's impending bankruptcy, he told an aide, without a hint of sarcasm, "The world is about to end."[28]

On Monday, September 15, Lehman Brothers officially became the

The Dangers of Credit Default Swaps

Brooksley Born, head of the government agency Commodity Futures Trading Commission [CFTC], was one of the few economists who recognized the hazards of credit default swaps. According to Born, the CDS market was vulnerable to fraud and manipulation because, "We had no regulation. No federal or state public official had any idea what was going on in those markets. . . . [We] didn't truly know the dangers in the market because it was a dark market. There was no transparency." In 1999 Born approached Congress with a plan to regulate CDSs, but she ran into fierce resistance from Chairman of the Federal Reserve Alan Greenspan and Secretary of the Treasury Robert Rubin. As a result, Congress took the extraordinary step of passing legislation that prohibited the CFTC from regulating the CDS market. Within days, Born resigned from her post.

In 2008 Born's predictions proved correct. As she told the TV show *Frontline*, "it became obvious as Lehman Brothers failed, as AIG suddenly appeared to be on the brink of tremendous defaults and turned out had been a major credit default swap dealer and needed hundreds of billions of dollars to keep it alive, the contagion in the marketplace from those failures brought many, many of our biggest financial services companies to the brink of collapse. And it was very frightening."

Quoted in PBS, "Interview: Brooksley Born," *Frontline*, August 28, 2009. www.pbs.org.

largest bankruptcy filing in US history. Worldwide financial markets responded in panic. The stock market on Wall Street dropped over five hundred points, losing about 4.5 percent of its total value. The stock markets in Tokyo and Hong Kong slid nearly 6 percent.

Bailout at AIG

Investors feared that companies that had been selling CDSs for years would be forced to pay off the insurance-like contracts on securities that had lost much of their value. The situation was particularly dire at AIG, which alone held $441 billion in CDC debt by this time. Federal officials feared that if AIG collapsed, it would set off a chain reaction that might bring down the economic system of the entire world. The complicated financial problems were difficult for many to understand, including the president. As Paulson remembers, a frustrated George W. Bush "found it hard to believe that an insurance company could be so systemically important."[29]

It was AIG's insurance business that connected it to so many aspects of the economy. In 2008 the company had more than 81 million life insurance policies valued at $1.9 trillion globally. People who own life insurance policies can cash them in for the amount they have paid over the years. If policyholders lost faith in AIG and rushed to cash in their policies all at once, it would be like a massive bank run. The entire life insurance industry could collapse. In addition, banks throughout the world bought CDSs from AIG. If these were not paid off, it would immediately cause hundreds of banks to shut down or borrow money to cover their losses. This would have forced surviving banks to drastically reduce the number of loans made to average citizens and small business.

On the afternoon of September 15, 2008, Moody's downgraded AIG's credit rating by three levels, causing the company's stock to drop a further 60 percent. The ratings downgrade meant AIG was obligated to raise as much as $75 billion for collateral to cover its CDSs.

On Tuesday, September 16, the Federal Reserve announced it would rescue AIG with an initial bailout of $85 billion. In exchange, the Federal Reserve received a 79 percent ownership stake in AIG. This meant the government could make major decisions at AIG, including hiring and firing management and selling off its numerous assets. This was an unprecedented move because the Federal Reserve is prohibited by law from owning a private company. However, the situation was so dire that few public officials protested the move.

The day after the AIG bailout was announced, the stock market continued its downward slide, losing 449 points. However, much of that loss was erased the following day when the federal government announced it would bail out the banks that were losing billions.

Troubled Assets Relief

On Thursday, September 18, Paulson, Federal Reserve chairman Ben Bernanke, and Bush approved a plan for a $700 billion bailout. This number was four times the $175 billion the Pentagon spent on the war on terror that year. When Bernanke presented the legislation to leaders in Congress he warned, "If we don't do this, we may not have an economy on Monday."[30] The proposal was written into legislation called the Emergency Economic Stabilization Act and passed by Congress on

Federal Reserve chairman Ben Bernanke (pictured) joined President George W. Bush and Treasury Secretary Henry Paulson in approving a $700 billion bank bailout in 2008. Bernanke warned that failure to approve the bailout could be ruinous for the economy.

October 3. The stabilization act established the Troubled Assets Recovery Program (TARP), which created funds to buy toxic mortgage-backed securities. While these securities were not worth much, they still had some value. Officials believed that if the mortgage-backed securities were held for several years, their value would increase. In addition, $115 billion was used to buy stock in AIG and eight banks including Goldman Sachs, JPMorgan, Citigroup, and Bank of America. When investors realized the government would not let these banks fail, stock prices went up.

As 2008 ended, a clear picture of the financial meltdown emerged. Twenty-six banks had failed in the United States, while the federal government was forced to purchase stock in 208 banks plus AIG. The Dow Jones Industrial Average was down 38 percent for the year. This was the Dow's worst performance since 1931, the second year of the Great Depression.

Beyond Wall Street, a record number of people were losing their jobs as the economy slowed. In 2004 the unemployment rate had been 3.9 percent. By 2008 that number was 7.2 percent. When Bush was asked to evaluate the economic scene he said, "I'm not really happy about the fact that there have been excesses in the financial markets which are affecting hard-working people."[31] As the figures showed, there was enough economic unhappiness in 2008 to spread from the White House to Wall Street to Main Street.

Chapter 3

Troubles on Main Street

On September 24, 2008, George W. Bush gave a televised speech, addressing the people of the United States and many worried investors throughout the world. Speaking of the financial crash, which had begun earlier in the month, Bush called the preceding weeks "extraordinary," and added, ". . . many Americans have felt anxiety about their finances and their future. I understand their worry and their frustration."[32]

Bush told Americans that the federal government was prepared to spend $700 billion taxpayer dollars to save the economy. Most of the money would go to purchasing toxic assets, stocks, and CDSs from the same financial institutions that had brought the world economy to the brink. Bush noted, "[I] understand the frustration of responsible Americans who pay their mortgages on time, file their tax returns every April 15th, and are reluctant to pay the cost of excesses on Wall Street."[33]

The morning after Bush's speech, those frustrations erupted in a public backlash that spilled into the streets. In more than one hundred American cities members of labor unions and grassroots political organizations like Democracy Now and USAction carried signs and chanted slogans that condemned politicians and bankers. The largest protest was on Wall Street where over one thousand people gathered at 4 p.m. when the banks and brokerage firms were closing for the night. Alan Charney, program director of USAction, summed up the attitude of the Wall Street protestors: "The people we entrusted to run our economy have failed us. We can no longer trust them to get us out of this financial mess. [The government should] put Main Street first."[34]

The Credit Crunch

Despite the protests, average citizens had little influence over the practices of Wall Street financial institutions. By early 2009 big banks had nearly stopped lending to individuals, new businesses, and small companies. This created what Tim Geithner, the new secretary of the treasury, called a "credit crunch."[35] During this period, even those with good credit histories found it difficult to borrow money for homes, cars, furniture, appliances, and other products. Economist Stephanie Kelton explains why this hurt the entire economy: "Spending is the lifeblood of our economy. Without it, there would be no sales, and without sales, no profits and no reason for any private firm to produce anything for the marketplace. . . . [One] person's spending becomes another person's income. . . . [Spending] creates income, income creates sales, and sales create jobs."[36]

With dropping sales and no available credit, business owners found it difficult to obtain loans. This money was needed to expand operations, hire new employees or, for some, simply to remain in business. Figures show that by mid-2009 lending to small businesses was down $113 billion from peak levels two years earlier. Prior to the recession, the economic activity of small businesses made up nearly 40 percent of the gross national product. And small businesses employed about half of America's workforce. In addition, small businesses in the United States have long been considered some of the most innovative in the world. Major corporations such as Apple, McDonalds, and Starbucks all started out as small businesses.

Unemployment

As the effects of the credit crunch rippled through society, unemployment increased dramatically. In December 2008, 681,000 Americans lost their jobs. In January 2009 the United States lost over 740,000 jobs, the largest monthly decline in sixty years. Unemployment rose to 8 percent. Things were little better in March. By the end of 2009 more than 6 million people had lost their jobs and unemployment had climbed to 10 percent.

Buying Appliances

President Obama's Recovery Act was meant to stimulate the economy, encourage job growth, and promote energy efficiency. In 2010 a $300 million program, which some called "Dollars for Dishwashers," encouraged home owners to trade in their old appliances for new energy-efficient models. Reporter Michael Grabell describes the success of the program:

> In many states, where the rebate was a generous $100 to $250, the rebates went like hotcakes. Texas opened its website and phone lines at 7:00 A.M. and handed out the last of its $20 million lot by 2:30 P.M. Minnesota burned through 25,000 rebates on the first day. Iowa's disappeared in eight hours. . . .
>
> By June 2011, consumers had bought 1.4 million appliances, 166,000 heating and air-conditioning units, and 30,000 water heaters. With most of the money spent, the program had generated $1.9 billion in sales. . . . On a visit to General Electric's Appliance Park campus in Louisville, Vice President [Joe] Biden noted that the sales of dishwashers had increased by 20 percent because of the rebates. Sales of clothes washers had more than doubled, causing GE to hire 137 employees to meet the demand.

Michael Grabell, *Money Well Spent?*, New York: PublicAffairs, 2012, p. 167.

Many workers who were affected by layoffs qualified for unemployment benefits. This is money paid by state and the federal governments to people who become unemployed through no fault of their own.

However, in economically hard-hit states like Ohio, unemployment compensation was only about $1,300 per month—equal to a typical monthly mortgage payment. At $15,600 per year, unemployment compensation was well below the average personal income at the time, which was more than $39,000 for men and $26,500 for women.

As the pool of unemployed workers expanded, many formerly middle-class people fell into poverty. According to a 2009 study by Rutgers University, 70 percent of those who lost their jobs in the recession were forced to spend their retirement funds, while 56 percent borrowed money from family or friends. Around 45 percent were forced to live off their credit cards. People facing these hardships struggled to get by using various strategies: 42 percent skimped on needed medical care, 20 percent were forced to move in with family or friends, and a similar number visited charity soup kitchens for meals.

Unemployment was not only bad for finances but for mental health as well. According to numerous studies, people who have been unemployed for more than six months show signs of depression, anxiety, and stress. Some unemployed people binge on food and alcohol, gain weight, lose sleep, and even commit suicide. According to psychotherapist Robert L. Leahy, "Being unemployed is actually one of the most difficult, most devastating experiences that people go through."[37]

Unemployment hurt even those who kept their jobs. According to business consultant Diane Hamilton, "When coworkers are laid off, those that remain must pick up the slack, meaning longer hours, harder work and less pay. Although corporations may show some profits during these times, it often comes from employee cuts or reduced wages for those who remain. Fear of job loss may leave employees feeling like they are at the mercy of their employers."[38]

Collapse in the Auto Industry

In January 2009 Barack Obama was sworn in as America's forty-fourth president. From his first day in office, Obama had to confront numerous daunting economic problems. Beyond the unemployment numbers, home values had plunged 25 percent from their 2006 high. More

Workers build cars at a General Motors assembly plant in Michigan. In 2009, as part of a deal to keep GM in business, the company laid off forty-seven thousand workers, closed five manufacturing plants, ended production of three car models, and shut down 40 percent of its car dealerships.

than 70 percent of home buyers were ineligible for refinancing, and the number of unsold homes was skyrocketing. In California, Nevada, Arizona, and Florida, the housing situation was even worse.

Problems in the housing market magnified troubles in the auto industry. In the years leading up to the recession, millions of people bought cars by refinancing their homes or taking out home equity loans. When these sources of credit were no longer available, the Big Three auto makers in Detroit—General Motors (GM), Ford, and Chrysler—faced bankruptcy. At the end of 2008, car sales had plunged 32 percent from the previous year. General Motors, the world's second largest car maker, lost $18 billion. Ford and Chrysler faced losses of $12 billion each.

The Big Three car makers had been central to the American economy since the early 1900s, and General Motors was the biggest company in the world during most of the twentieth century. By the 2000s the Big Three, together with their thousands of parts suppliers, provided decent wages to over 3 million middle-class Americans. By contrast, Apple, which was the largest American corporation in 2012, employed about 43,000 in the United States.

To prevent the Big Three from declaring bankruptcy in late December 2008, the Bush administration provided emergency loans of around $9 billion to GM and $4 billion to Chrysler. (Ford refused government loans and managed to turn a profit in 2009.) Barack Obama, then president-elect, supported the Bush loans, saying the money was "a necessary step to help avoid a collapse in our auto industry that would have devastating consequences for our economy and our workers."[39] However, by the following February GM and Chrysler were again on the verge of collapse. This prompted the new Obama administration to provide a second bailout, somewhat larger than the first.

In July 2009 the Obama administration worked out a deal to keep GM in business. General Motors filed for bankruptcy, and the US Treasury promised it would inject $30 billion into the company. In exchange, the government received 60 percent ownership in GM, a controversial move. The government had never taken ownership of a private business as large as General Motors. No existing laws or policies dictated how the Treasury Department should run a car company. This prompted conservative columnists and talk show hosts to refer to GM by a new name. As policy analyst Peter Flaherty noted, General Motors is "now forever known as 'Government Motors.'"[40] Obama responded to critics, saying: "What we are not doing—what I have no interest in doing—is running GM. . . . When a difficult decision has to be made on matters like where to open a new plant or what type of new car to make, the new GM, not the United States government, will make that decision."[41]

As part of the bankruptcy deal, GM laid off forty-seven thousand employees, closed down five manufacturing plants, and stopped production of its renowned Pontiac, Hummer, and Saturn models. In addition, GM shut down 40 percent of its car dealerships, many of them in small towns where they were the economic mainstays. Chrysler, which was a smaller company, cut three thousand manufacturing jobs, ceased production on three models, and shut down 25 percent of its dealerships.

Recovery and Reinvestment

With unemployment reaching a crisis level, Obama presented a plan called the American Recovery and Reinvestment Act to address the economic problems of average citizens. The act set aside $787 billion to stimulate the economy. After it was approved by Congress in February 2009 it was widely referred to as the Recovery Act or simply the Stimulus.

The Recovery Act used taxpayer money to increase employment in sectors such as education, construction, health, and green energy. Around $47 billion went to repair and update what is called infrastructure: bridges, roads, water systems, sewers, and buses, trains, and other mass transit. Another $21 billion went to subsidize health insurance for laid-off workers; $55 billion went to schools to prevent cuts in education; $40 billion went to energy efficiency and renewable energy programs.

Cash for Clunkers

One of the most popular parts of the Recovery Act was known as Cash for Clunkers. This program was put in place to help increase auto sales, which had fallen to their lowest monthly levels since 1982. Officially called the Car Allowance Rebate System (CARS), Cash for Clunkers provided $3,500 to $4,500 to anyone trading in older, high-fuel-consumption vehicles for new, energy-efficient models.

Cash for Clunkers, which began July 1, 2009, set off a buying frenzy at car dealerships, which had been empty for months. At the Ford dealership in Rochester, New York, buyers lined up before dawn on the first day of the program, and some were still closing deals at 3 a.m. the following morning. Nationwide, in the first four days of the program, 250,000 people bought cars. This created its own problems; the government computer system set up to handle the paperwork repeatedly

Unemployment Stories

The media website Gawker hosted a series called "Unemployment Stories" in which people described their unemployment hardships. The following was written by an anonymous college graduate in her mid-twenties who had obtained four degrees:

> One month after graduation, the only jobs I could actually find [were] a telemarketing job and as a companion for an elderly male. The part-time telemarketing job was for an accountant. I sat in a room with 10 other employees (all over 70), where we had to go through the phone book to ask people if they needed accountant services. It paid minimum wage/no benefits or job security. . . . It was demoralizing and depressing. . . . Anyways, that was in 2008. Since then, I've found work as a hostess (with high school students, making minimum wage and only being guaranteed 10 hours a week). This job was extremely demoralizing because what I made in wages went directly to the gas to get there, the boss watched us like a hawk and had us doing twenty different tasks for minimum wage. . . . Since 2008, I haven't had health insurance, am living at home, I have had about 5 or 6 different jobs that have not had benefits, stable hours, have had reduced pay, and have endured horrible abuse. . . . I wish I had never gone to university in the first place and had just gotten a tech degree at a community college.

Hamilton Nolan, "Unemployment Stories, Vol. Ten," Gawker, October 1, 2012. http://gawker.com.

froze, timed out, and crashed. In Washington, DC, the Department of Transportation had to bring in one hundred employees to handle phone calls, while the computer company Oracle continually upgraded the computer system.

The Obama administration expected the money set aside for the program to last until November. However, Cash for Clunkers was so successful that funding was exhausted in one week. Car dealers and customers frantically called their representatives to get the program extended. Within days Congress added another $2 billion from the Recovery Act.

By the time the Cash for Clunkers program ended on August 24, over 680,000 vehicles had been sold. This prompted the Big Three to reopen manufacturing plants that had been shut down for months. General Motors increased production by 60,000 vehicles and called over 1,350 employees back to work. Similar increases were seen by Ford and Chrysler. Cash for Clunkers also helped Americans working at foreign-owned plants. Hyundai hired over 3,500 workers at its Montgomery, Alabama, plant, and Honda increased production in Ohio. In late 2009 the White House Council of Economic Advisors estimated the Cash for Clunkers program created or saved 70,000 jobs. According to Transportation Secretary Ray LaHood, the program, "stimulated the economy, generated jobs, and helped consumers dump their gas guzzlers. And it's taken toxic greenhouse gases out of the air to improve the environment."[42]

Dollars for Dishwashers

Cash for Clunkers was so successful with consumers that the Obama administration reshaped the plan to cover major appliances. Known as Dollars for Dishwashers, the program was designed to encourage people to replace old, inefficient refrigerators, electric ranges, water heaters, and dishwashers with new energy-efficient ones.

While Dollars for Dishwashers and Cash for Clunkers undoubtedly stimulated sales, analysts were divided as to the overall success of the Recovery Act. When Obama signed the Recovery Act, he predicted that it would help the GNP grow by 4.6 percent and reduce unemployment to

6 percent. However, according to the nonpartisan Congressional Budget Office (CBO), by the end of 2010 the GNP grew about 2 percent, while unemployment was stuck at over 8 percent. According to the CBO, the stimulus created between 1.6 million and 4.6 million jobs.

A "Cancerous Spread" of Vacant Homes

Despite some improving economic numbers, vast portions of the American landscape were transformed by the Great Recession. From New Jersey to California, once-thriving neighborhoods emptied as banks foreclosed on homes. According to the news agency Reuters, more than 18.6 million homes were left empty in the United States by 2010. Some were older homes in big cities like Newark, Detroit, Cleveland, and Chicago. Others were large and luxurious new homes, built in housing developments in California, Arizona, and Florida.

Wherever they were located, abandoned homes quickly deteriorated. Houses with broken windows, dead lawns, missing shingles, and peeling paint blighted hundreds of neighborhoods. The houses also attracted criminals, including gang members who used the homes to hide drugs, weapons, and stolen property. It was common for vandals to break into houses and strip them of kitchen cabinets, countertops, furnaces, sinks, toilets, doors, appliances, and copper pipes and wires. In warm climates people even dug up the palm and citrus trees in yards of abandoned houses.

In Cleveland, Ohio, an estimated twelve thousand homes sat vacant and abandoned—one in every ten houses in the city. Newspaper ads offered three-bedroom homes for $7,000 that had once sold for $150,000. Jim Rokakis, the treasurer for Cleveland's Cuyahoga County, placed the blame on the subprime lending frenzy: "Wall Street strategies that made the cycle of no-money-down, no-questions-asked lending possible have sucked the life out of my city."[43]

When homes are abandoned, cities can no longer collect property taxes from the owners. In little more than two years, between the middle of 2007 and the end of 2009, cities and states lost $917 million in property taxes because of foreclosures. This money was needed

Abandoned and vandalized, foreclosed houses blight a neighborhood in Cleveland, Ohio, in 2008. Vacant, foreclosed homes in older neighborhoods deteriorated quickly; some provided haven for gangs and drug dealers.

for police and fire protection, libraries, schools, sanitation, and other services. In Cleveland, officials place the cost of simply tearing down all the vacant homes at $100 million.

Those who remained in their homes saw their property values drop drastically. As Cleveland *Plain Dealer* columnist Brent Larkin describes the situation, "[The city] is threatened by the cancerous spread of vacant and abandoned houses. . . . Empty houses are destroying a once-great city from within. Some neighborhoods are almost lost. Others aren't far behind."[44]

In Detroit, the city was left with an estimated thirty thousand abandoned homes and other buildings, many of which were taken over by drug dealers and other criminals. Arson was another major problem. In 2011 the Detroit Fire Department put out thirty thousand fires, about half of them set by vandals in vacant homes. Detroit's empty neighborhoods had even become dumping grounds for the dead. In 2012 the Detroit police department reported finding about one body a month left among the urban waste. According to Detroit police officer John Garner, "You can shoot a person, dump a body and it may just go unsolved because of the time it may take for the corpse to be found."[45]

Long-Lasting Consequences

Although the Great Recession officially ended in 2009 when the overall economy began to improve, things remained bleak on Main Street. In August 2010 one home in America was being foreclosed on every thirteen seconds—more than six thousand a day. Unemployment remained stubbornly high, especially for recent college graduates. More than 19 percent of twenty-five-year-old college grads were out of work. About 38 percent of young graduates with bachelor degrees were under employed. This translated to 760,000 out of 2 million grads working at jobs that did not require a degree.

By September 2012, five years after the Great Recession began, the national unemployment rate was 7.9 percent, with higher numbers in states such as California (10 percent), Nevada (12 percent), and Michigan (9.8 percent). Nearly 50 million Americans were living in poverty, up from 37 million in 2006. While the United States managed to avoid another Great Depression in the 2000s, there is little doubt that the Great Recession had long-lasting consequences. Foreclosures, unemployment, underemployment, and homelessness took not only an economic toll on the country but an emotional one as well.

Chapter 4

A Global Recession

The Great Recession was triggered when financial institutions on Wall Street accumulated billions of dollars worth of toxic debt that they could not repay. This debt was traced to subprime loans, mortgage-backed securities, and credit default swaps. To prevent a collapse of the economic system, the toxic debt accumulated by troubled financial and insurance firms was paid off by the federal government with about $2 trillion in taxpayer dollars.

The economic problems that set off the recession in the United States quickly rippled through the world economy. Major banks failed in England and Germany because of their ties to Wall Street. In late 2007 Sachsen LB, the state bank of Saxony, Germany, nearly collapsed when the value plunged on the American mortgage-backed securities it had purchased. Several other state banks failed for similar reasons and all had to be rescued by the German government.

Germany was one of the wealthiest countries in the world and was able to absorb the huge debts created by the mortgage meltdown. Other countries, such as Iceland, Greece, Spain, Portugal, and Ireland, were not in the same position. These countries lacked the financial resources to pay off their debts when the economy slowed. For example, banks in Ireland created debt equal to more than 25 times the country's annual tax revenues. By way of comparison, the approximately $2 trillion financial collapse in the United States was about equal to all federal taxes collected in one year.

Icelandic Economics

Iceland is one of the best examples of a country imitating the practices of Wall Street and failing spectacularly during the Great Recession. A remote country of 320,000 people, Iceland is the size of Kentucky and is located on the Arctic Ocean. For centuries the nation's main economic activity was centered on the fishing industry, and the nation prospered as a result. Residents of the sparsely populated island were among the most well-educated and prosperous in the world. However, around 2003, thousands of young Icelanders chose to abandon fishing for jobs in the banking industry located in the capital city of Reykjavik. As financial journalist Michael Lewis writes, "An entire nation without immediate experience or even distant memory of high finance had gazed upon the example of Wall Street and said, 'We can do that.'"[46] This eventually led to a total collapse of the nation's banking system, which economist Paul Krugman called "one of the greatest economic disaster stories of all time."[47]

Iceland's move into the world of high finance began in 2002 when the government-owned central bank was privatized. Before this move, the bank mainly served the needs of Icelanders. The bank broke up into three privately owned institutions, Landsbanki, Kaupthing, and Glitnir. The new owners of the banks—and their friends— set up private financial companies. According to journalists Robert Wade and Silla Sigurgeirsdóttir, "None of these newly minted bankers had much experience in national, let alone international, finance."[48]

Because they had been owned by the government, Moody's gave Iceland banks high credit ratings. This allowed the new private bankers to borrow billions. The money was used to buy up businesses across the globe, including a British soccer team, Norwegian banks, Indian power plants, and an 8 percent stake in American Airlines. In addition, Iceland's investors bought mortgage-backed securities and credit default swaps on Wall Street. With the worldwide economy soaring in the mid-2000s, the value of these assets rapidly increased. Icelandic banks used this equity to borrow even more money, mainly from banks in the United Kingdom and the Netherlands.

Between 2003 and 2006, the value of Iceland's three main banks jumped from a few billion dollars to over $140 billion. This figure was more than 800 percent of Iceland's gross domestic product and was the most rapid economic expansion of any banking system in history. As

"I Feel Like I'm Dead"

As Greek politicians fought to save their country's economy, they instituted austerity measures that caused numerous hardships for average citizens. Andy Dabilis, a journalist for the Greek Reporter website, describes how the recession affected Anastasia Karagaitanaki, 57, a former cafe owner in Thessaloniki, Greece:

> After losing her business to the financial crisis, she now sleeps on a daybed next to the refrigerator in her mother's kitchen and depends on charity for food and insulin for her diabetes. "I feel like my life has slipped through my hands," said Karagaitanaki, whose brother also shares the one-bedroom apartment. "I feel like I'm dead." For thousands of Greeks like Karagaitanaki, the fabric of middle-class life is unraveling. Teachers, salaries slashed by a third, are stealing electricity. Families in once-stable neighborhoods are afraid to leave their homes because of rising street crime.
>
> Karagaitanaki's family can't afford gas to heat their home this winter and will rely on electric blankets in the chilly northern Greek city. They live on the 785 euros ($1,027) a month their mother collects monthly from their late father's pension. Two years ago, Karagaitanaki sold her jewelry for 3,000 euros, which she gave to her two sons. Her blood sugar is rising because she can't afford the meat and vegetables her doctor recommends and instead eats rice and beans she gets from the Greek Orthodox Church. "We are waiting every month for my mother's pension," Karagaitanaki said. "If my mother dies, what can I do? Everyone here is dependent on their parents' pensions."

Andy Dabilis, "Austerity, Depression, Crime Weigh Down Greeks," Greek Reporter, December 6, 2012. http://greece.greekreporter.com.

they grew, the banks opened branches throughout Europe, the United States, South America, and elsewhere. The growth of the banking industry also attracted foreign investors. German banks deposited $21 billion in Icelandic banks; Netherlands, $305 million; and Sweden, $400 million. Bankers in the United Kingdom deposited $30 billion. This money came from individual savings accounts, pension funds, hospitals, and universities.

Even as the banks were financing the purchase of international assets, they were also loaning Icelanders money to buy stocks, real estate, and cars. By 2006 average Icelanders were three times as wealthy as they had been in 2003. During this period Iceland's real estate prices tripled, and the value of its national stock market increased 900 percent.

Iceland's economic activity created thousands of millionaires virtually overnight. In a nation where almost everyone had previously been middle-class, people began importing expensive cars and drinking champagne. As Wade and Sigurgeirsdóttir explain: "Reykjavik's shops brimmed with luxury goods, its restaurants made London look cheap, and SUVs choked its narrow streets. Icelanders were the happiest people in the world, according to an international study in 2006." [49]

While few Icelanders questioned their economic good fortune, outsiders were perplexed. In the world of high finance, it was extremely unusual for previously unknown businesspeople to buy millions of shares of major corporations like American Airlines. One London firm decided to hire financial investigators to examine Iceland's skyrocketing financial system. Lewis describes what was discovered:

> The investigators produced a chart detailing a byzantine web of interlinked entities that boiled down to this: a handful of guys in Iceland [banks] who had no experience in finance were taking out tens of billions of dollars in short-term loans from abroad. They were then relending this money to themselves and their friends to buy assets—the banks, soccer teams, etc. Since the entire world's assets were rising—thanks in part to people like those Icelandic [guys] paying crazy prices for them—they appeared to be making money. [50]

Iceland's move into the world of high finance led to economic disaster. By 2008 the country's once-vibrant economy, largely based on the fishing industry, had collapsed. The collapse affected all segments of the population, including workers in a fish processing facility (pictured).

The Kitchenware Revolution

The collapse of Iceland's economy was even faster than its rise. In mid-September 2008, after Wall Street giant Lehman Brothers failed, American banks stopped making short-term loans such as those used by Reykjavik bankers. Within a week, the credit crunch caused Iceland's three major banks to fail. The value of the Icelandic stock market fell by an astonishing 98 percent.

To prevent complete financial chaos, Iceland's government was forced to nationalize, or take over, the banks and used taxpayer funds to pay off the debts. In October, Iceland's 320,000 citizens discovered they were responsible for $100 billion in losses, equal to about $300,000 for every man, woman, and child in the country. The debt was more than 850 percent of the Iceland's gross national product, or the value of all goods and services produced by the country for eight-and-a-half years.

The calamity caused the value of Iceland's monetary unit, the krona, to plummet by 50 percent. This meant the krona could purchase only half of what it had before. This made the foreign luxury goods in Iceland's stores impossibly expensive for almost everyone. In addition, housing values collapsed, and average incomes went into free fall. This left many Icelanders bankrupt. One of these was Klemens Thrastarson, a thirty-three-year-old journalist and homeowner. He stated, "If it reaches the point where the monthly installments from the housing loan will be equal to my paycheck, I would have no qualms about handing in the keys to my house, declare bankruptcy and perhaps leave the country."[51] Thrastarson was not alone. Within weeks of the financial meltdown, one-third of Icelanders told pollsters they were thinking about emigrating.

Icelanders reacted to the financial disaster with angry protests. Demonstrators of all ages gathered in Reykjavik's main square, made speeches, sang songs, and threw fruit and yogurt at Iceland's capital building, the Althingi. Because people were also banging pots and pans to make noise, the protests were called the Kitchenware Revolution. For months, the protestors assembled every Monday at Reykjavik's biggest movie theater to debate the situation and berate government officials, who were called in to explain themselves.

In March 2010, Icelanders held an election to vote on a measure called the Icesave Referendum. Icesave would have used taxpayer funds to bail out the big banks and repay billions in debt to other countries. The measure was rejected by 93 percent of the public, and the banks were allowed to fail. By refusing to pay off debts incurred by the financial system, Iceland's government had enough money to increase the budgets of social programs. Extra money was set aside for the unemployed and to provide relief to home owners struggling with their mortgages. Strict controls were put in place to prevent Icelandic companies from investing abroad. In addition, foreign investors were forbidden to take their money out of Iceland. As economist Krugman notes, "Where everyone else bailed out the bankers and made the public pay the price, Iceland let the banks go bust and actually expanded its social safety net. Where everyone else was fixated on trying to placate international investors, Iceland imposed temporary controls on the movement of capital [money] to give itself room to maneuver."[52]

By the end of 2010 Iceland's economy was steadily growing, and the nation emerged from recession. In the years that followed, unemployment declined and the standard of living for average Icelanders returned to 2003 levels.

Deficits and Spending in Greece

Iceland's economic complications occurred in the private sector during a short period of a few years. However, the challenges in Greece were created by high levels of government debt that had been growing for decades. And while Iceland's financial woes had little effect on other countries, this was not the case with Greece, whose economic problems threatened the world economy.

In 2010 Greece, with a population of 11 million, was part of the European Union (EU), an economic and political association formed in 1992. The EU is made up of twenty-seven nations, including the United Kingdom, Germany, France, Ireland, Italy, Poland, Bulgaria, Spain, and Sweden. With its interlinked financial systems, the European Union is considered the largest single economy in the world. Most nations in the union use the same currency, the euro. (In 2010, €1.00 was roughly equal to $1.25.)

Problems in Greece were traced to high levels of government spending, low levels of tax collection, and fraudulent bookkeeping. Problems began in 1999 when Greek officials misleadingly claimed that their budget shortfall, or deficit, was much smaller than it was. Deficits are created when governments spend more money than they collect in taxes. Money has to be borrowed to cover deficits and repaid with interest. Deficits become a problem when they grow so large that they cannot be repaid, which leaves an entire country facing bankruptcy, something that rarely happens.

European Day of Action and Solidarity

On November 14, 2012, millions of people protested and held strikes in twenty-three countries on what was called the European Day of Action and Solidarity. The demonstrations were particularly rowdy in Spain, Portugal, Greece, and Italy, where the harshest austerity measures had been instituted. Journalist Barbie Latza Nadeau describes the protests in Italy:

> Across Italy, an estimated 300,000 demonstrators took to the streets in 100 cities. Protesters broke windows and blocked the central train station in Naples. . . . In Florence, angry mobs plastered bank windows with rotten eggs and defaced the normally pristine city center with profane graffiti. In Pisa, a group of angry protesters briefly occupied the historic Leaning Tower of Pisa, hanging a sign that read "Rise Up. We are not paying for your Euro crisis."
>
> In Rome, glass shards littered busy thoroughfares and a thick cloud of toxic smoke from paper bombs and tear gas hung over the city center as thousands of uninhibited protesters—many wearing helmets and gas masks—threw glass bottles and broken cobblestones at riot police. At one point, police used an armored jeep to disperse the crowds before trapping a handful of violent protesters on a bridge over the dangerously flooded Tiber River. The students flung their helmets, bottles, and Molotov cocktails [gasoline bombs] into the water before finally giving up. More than a dozen police officers were injured in Rome and more than 60 protesters were detained.

Quoted in Barbie Latza Nadeau, "Europe's Day of Austerity Rage," *Daily Beast*, November 14, 2012. www.thedailybeast.com.

To hide the extent of Greece's deficit, its financial officials had used accounting tricks for decades. For example, one year huge military costs were left out of the budget. Another year it was billions spent on hospitals. Greece also worked with Wall Street firms, including Goldman Sachs and JPMorgan, to create complex financial products. These allowed Greece to hide its debt by keeping existing expenses off the books for ten years.

While the government was hiding its deficits, it was also spending at a rapid pace. In the early 2000s Greece increased the wages paid to government employees, including those who operated the state-run trains, schools, and hospitals. By 2008 the average government job paid three times more than a job in the private sector. In addition, retirement age for government workers was fifty-five for men, fifty for women. These people received pensions for the rest of their lives. This added an estimated $800 billion to the long-term deficit.

Greece's government also had a problem of widespread tax fraud. People who worked as salaried employees for large companies had taxes automatically taken from their paychecks every week. However, the large majority of Greeks were self-employed. They did not receive weekly paychecks with automatic deductions but were required to self-report their income to the government. And most people did not do so accurately. For example, according to government statistics, two-thirds of Greek doctors regularly lied about their income in order to avoid paying any income tax. And some surgeons making $1 million a year paid zero taxes. As an anonymous tax collector stated to Lewis, avoiding taxes "has become a cultural trait. The Greek people never learned to pay their taxes. And they never did because no one is punished. No one *has ever been* punished. It's a cavalier offence—like a gentleman not opening a door for a lady."[53]

Losing Trust

In October 2009 European Union officials finally exposed Greece's accounting and tax problems. The actual deficit was revealed to be over $400 billion, almost four times higher than previously stated. This deficit was one of the highest in the world relative to the country's gross domestic product. Greece was facing bankruptcy, but unlike Iceland, its problems threatened the entire European Union. Economist Hans-Werner Sinn explains:

> If Greece went bust, investors from all over the world could lose their trust in the stability of the weaker EU countries. In an extreme case, this could mean that they would immediately stop lending . . . which would increase the governments' budget deficits and make the public debt grow even faster. . . . [Other] endangered countries could include Ireland, Portugal, Spain, Belgium, or Italy, because they also have high [deficits].[54]

In May 2010, in order to prevent the economic problems from spreading, the European Union offered Greece emergency loans totaling $147 billion. In return, Greece was obligated to engage in what is called an austerity program, a plan to reduce the deficit through drastic wage and pension cuts, new corporate taxes, and much higher sales taxes. These measures were meant to save $30 billion by 2012.

Violent Protests

While the austerity measures helped restore investor confidence in the European Union, they generated widespread, often violent, street protests. The first nationwide strike began at midnight on May 5, 2010, when the austerity program went into effect. With workers on strike, airplane, train, and ferry traffic ceased, schools shut down, and most private businesses closed. Over 200,000 people gathered in the streets of Athens, and a large group of angry protestors tried to storm the country's parliament building. Riot police responded with tear gas and smoke bombs. The protests turned violent, and demonstrators lit trash cans on fire and threw rocks and bottles at police. A gasoline bomb was thrown into a bank building filled with employees who had come to work during the strike because they feared losing their jobs. While

Demonstrators and riot police clash in Greece during a nationwide strike in May 2010. The Greek government was forced to enact severe and unpopular austerity measures to avoid damage to the European Union, of which Greece is a member.

most of the workers escaped, two men and a woman who was four months pregnant died in the fire.

Periodic protests continued in Greece throughout 2011 and 2012 as new austerity measures were implemented. During this period over sixty-eight thousand small businesses shut down, and general unemployment rose to 25 percent. Jobless figures were 54 percent for those under the age of twenty-five. Millions who kept their jobs saw their pay cut to the minimum wage, which at the time was around €592 per month, or $740. While the demonstrations helped average Greeks express their displeasure, they also hurt the economy. About one in five jobs in Greece was based on tourism. However, in 2012 the number of tourists was down by 25 percent because of widely televised protests in the streets.

Experts predicted it might take more than a decade for Greece's economy to recover, but average Greeks held little hope for the future. According to researcher George Tzogopoulos, "I don't think there is a single Greek citizen who believes that things will be better. There is no money for people to spend."[55]

Interconnected Economies

At the end of 2012 Greece was among five EU nations dealing with severe debt crises. The others—Italy, Spain, Portugal, and Cyprus—imposed austerity measures which cut pensions and raised taxes. As with Greece, these measures, lowered worker income and living standards and increased unemployment and bankruptcies. The measures also generated protests and strikes in nations across Europe. One of the largest, the European Day of Action and Solidarity, occurred on November 14, 2012, when millions of demonstrators took to the streets in twenty-three EU countries.

Beyond Europe, there were fears that the ongoing recession might worsen economic problems in the United States as well. The European Union, with its population of 332 million, is the largest customer for US exports. It is also a major source of sales for leading American companies. For example, 40 percent of McDonald's global sales occur in Europe—more than the company generates in the United States. General Motors sold 1.7 million vehicles in Europe in 2011, one-fifth of its worldwide sales.

From the United States to Iceland and Italy, the twenty-first century economy is interconnected in countless ways. Economic activity travels nonstop across the Internet at the speed of light, between banks, corporations, government treasuries, and stock markets. The mistakes made by financial firms in Reykjavik might create banking problems in London that hurt profits at a car company in Detroit. Meanwhile, hundreds of millions of workers depend on jobs over which they have little control. Although economic activities will always rise and fall, never before have people in developed nations been so dependent on one another for their well-being.

Chapter 5

What Was the Impact of the Great Recession?

On September 20, 2010, the National Bureau of Economic Research (NBER) issued a report saying the Great Recession had officially ended as of June 2009. The bureau is made up of more than one thousand professors of economics and business, including twenty-two Nobel Prize winners. The bureau said the recession was the worst since World War II. It was also the deepest economic slowdown since the Great Depression in terms of job loss.

The NBER based its findings on economic indicators such as the gross national product, employment statistics, and industrial production. However, at the time of its announcement the recession had not ended for millions of people. As the report stated, the NBER "did not conclude that economic conditions since [June 2009] have been favorable or that the economy has returned to operating at normal capacity. Rather, the committee determined only that the recession ended and a recovery began in that month."[56]

By definition a recession ends after employment grows by 1.5 percent and gross national product rises for two quarters. However, the financial meltdown of 2008 and the damage that followed left a weakened economy for average Americans. In September 2012, four years after the financial meltdown on Wall Street, more than 8 million Americans were unemployed. Of that group, 5.4 million had been out of work for at least six months, while 750,000 were completely destitute.

Those who kept their jobs often found their workplace permanently transformed. In the wake of the recession, many companies cut their payrolls, lowered wages, and reduced benefits such as medical insurance. This created what economists call wage stagnation, meaning that average workers could expect to see little increase in their paychecks in the coming years.

While wages were stagnant, millions were left with huge debts after the crash. This was particularly true for people whose mortgages were underwater; that is, they owed more on their mortgages than their homes were worth. By 2010, 12 million mortgages in the United States—25 percent—were underwater. In some areas the figures were even worse. In Nevada, 61 percent of mortgages were underwater. In Florida and Arizona that number was around 45 percent, while in Georgia and Michigan it was about 37 percent.

Wall Street Reform

The impact of the recession on average Americans prompted widespread calls for financial reform in Washington, DC. In July 2010 Congress addressed some of the problems that caused the economic crisis by passing the Dodd-Frank Wall Street Reform and Consumer Protection Act. The bill, commonly referred to as Dodd-Frank, is named after its sponsors, Massachusetts representative Barney Frank and Connecticut senator Christopher Dodd.

Dodd-Frank is a complex, twenty-three-hundred-page bill with reforms and regulations that touch nearly every aspect of the financial industry. According to the Senate Banking Committee, the bill addresses the problem of "too big to fail" banks and "[e]nds the possibility that taxpayers will be asked to write a check to bail out financial firms that threaten the economy by . . . establishing rigorous standards and supervision to protect the economy and American consumers, investors and businesses."[57]

Dodd-Frank also created a Financial Stability Oversight Council to oversee the financial services market and identify and regulate products that might threaten economic stability. If such a council had existed in

Thousands of job seekers attend a job fair in Georgia in 2009. Millions of Americans lost their jobs during the Great Recession. Thousands of people who kept their jobs were forced to accept lower wages and reduced benefits.

the early 2000s, it might have put an end to the sale of mortgage-backed securities and credit default swaps, which had touched off the economic crisis. The bill also contains a provision called the Volcker rule, named after former Federal Reserve chairman Paul Volcker. This rule was written to prevent banks from engaging in risky trades of stocks and other financial instruments.

Dodd-Frank tightened lending standards in the subprime mortgage industry to end the practice of providing mortgages to low-doc and no-doc customers. This returned the lending industry to the strictures of an era when mortgage applicants had had to prove that their incomes would allow them to repay their loans.

Executive Pay

As Dodd-Frank was being written, Dodd added a rule that limited executive pay and bonuses at firms that accepted government bailouts.

This was in response to reports that the failed insurance company AIG had paid $165 million in bonuses to 418 employees after it had received a $200 billion government bailout.

Before the financial meltdown, few people had questioned executive pay on Wall Street. However, after the Great Recession, the public was angered by the huge sums given to corporate chiefs whose companies had failed so spectacularly. For example, AIG FP head Joseph Cassano, who was responsible for selling hundreds of billions of dollars' worth of toxic credit default swaps, was paid a $34 million bonus when he retired in March 2008. Richard Fuld, CEO of Lehman Brothers, earned over $500 million in the six years prior to Lehman's bankruptcy. In 2009 the monthly magazine *Condé Nast Portfolio* placed Fuld's name at the top of their list of the "Worst American CEOs of All Time," writing, "Fuld's reckless risk-taking may have been typical of Wall Street, but his refusal to acknowledge that his firm was in trouble—and take the steps necessary to save it—was beyond the pale."[58]

Angelo Mozilo, the head of Countrywide Financial, was number two on *Portfolio's* list. Mozilo earned about $600 million while providing toxic subprime mortgages that, according to *Portfolio*, "would ultimately bring down the economy."[59] Mozilo was prosecuted by the government for fraud and other crimes but escaped jail time. He was fined $67.5 million, but one-third of that amount was paid by Countrywide.

Mozilo, Fuld, and Cassano were among the twenty top financial managers who received a total of $11.6 billion in pay as the economy plunged. While Dodd-Frank attempted to address this issue, many institutions such as Goldman Sachs and JPMorgan returned their bailout funds. This freed the companies from the executive pay rules in the bill. Business professor Edward E. Lawler III criticizes this trend in the corporate world:

> Considerable research shows that today's high level of executive compensation has created an enormous . . . gap between the top earners in the country and the rest of the population. Compensation has become so high that it significantly affects the profitability of even relatively large corporations. Perhaps

less frequently noted are the pay plans that . . . can lead people to take risky and even illegal actions in order to make their pay-for-performance compensation pay off.[60]

Consumer Protection

With public fury at Wall Street at an all-time high, Dodd-Frank included measures to shield average Americans from harmful banking practices. The act created the Consumer Financial Protection Bureau (CFPB). One goal of this new government agency was to provide fairness and clarity to the loan process. This meant banishing long, complicated loan application forms filled with convoluted legal language, what Harvard Law School professor Elizabeth Warren labels "tricks and traps buried in fine print."[61] As a result of Dodd-Frank, loan consumers would be provided with a complete and understandable estimate of the costs. This was meant to prevent consumers from unknowingly signing up for risky loans, such as adjustable rate mortgages with steeply rising interest rates.

Whatever its goals, the Dodd-Frank Act and the Consumer Financial Protection Bureau met strong opposition. Powerful politicians and figures on Wall Street argued that the regulations would lower profits, harm economic recovery, and increase unemployment. As former speaker of the House Newt Gingrich said in 2011, Dodd-Frank is "a devastatingly bad bill [that is] killing small banks, killing small business, killing the housing industry."[62]

Banking industry groups such as the Financial Services Roundtable as well as banks including Wells Fargo, JP Morgan Chase, and Citigroup spent around $100 million lobbying Congress to repeal or make drastic changes to Dodd-Frank. On the one-year anniversary of the bill, the Republican-controlled House voted to weaken Dodd-Frank and abolish the CFPB. The move was not approved by the Senate and did not become law. However, the House did succeed in cutting the budgets of banking regulators tasked with writing four hundred complex new Dodd-Frank rules that would regulate the financial industry. By 2012 only one hundred of the rules had been written. Several aspects of

Harvard Law School professor Elizabeth Warren explains why she was a leading advocate for the creation of the Consumer Financial Protection Bureau (CFPB):

> After the crash, it was clear that restoring a working consumer credit market was among the most urgent challenges. The broken consumer credit market had to be repaired by making sure that consumers had the right information and could use it effectively. . . .
>
> The new CFPB was designed to level the playing field for small players—families, students, seniors, community banks, credit unions, small businesses. It aimed to cut complexity out of the system, mowing down the fine print that hid bad surprises, using easy-to-read forms, and getting rid of tricky language. It aimed to let people make apples-to-apples comparisons when shopping for financial products, so people could evaluate three mortgages head-to-head or the terms of three student loan offers. The new agency was also designed to be a cop on the beat to make sure that even the biggest banks follow the law. . . .
>
> The CFPB is also already helping military servicemembers better navigate the financial challenges of multiple moves and deployments and passing on targeted information to protect seniors, students, and young families about their financial options.

Elizabeth Warren, "Tricks, Traps, and Accountability," *Huffington Post*, July 23, 2012. www.huffingtonpost.com.

the law were also challenged in court. As Frank says, his bill was "facing a death through a thousand cuts."[63]

Occupy Wall Street

While politicians, bankers, and regulators argued over Dodd-Frank, ongoing economic problems ignited some of the largest demonstrations seen in the United States in a generation. The Occupy Wall Street movement began around the three-year anniversary of the massive financial bailout. The demonstration was initiated by a Canadian activist magazine, *Adbusters*, with a circulation of about one hundred thousand worldwide. The *Adbusters* website describes itself as "a global network of culture jammers and creatives working to change the way information flows, the way corporations wield power, and the way meaning is produced in our society."[64] Two months before the demonstration, word of the gathering was spread through social media sites such as Twitter and Facebook.

On September 17, 2011, about one thousand peaceful protesters gathered in Zuccotti Park, located in Wall Street's financial district. The Occupy protesters adopted the slogan "We Are the 99 Percent." This was meant to distinguish average citizens from the perceived 1 percent of people who grew wealthy from financial activities on Wall Street. The Occupy Wall Street website explains the meaning of the slogan: "We are the 99 percent. We are getting kicked out of our homes. We are forced to choose between groceries and rent. We are denied quality medical care. We are suffering from environmental pollution. We are working long hours for little pay and no rights, if we're working at all. We are getting nothing while the other 1 percent is getting everything. We are the 99 percent."[65]

The Occupy movement set up encampments in Zuccotti Park, which they renamed "Liberty Plaza." The park was divided into several areas. The camp, where people lived, was a jumble of tents, tarps, sleeping bags, and shopping bags. The comfort center provided free blankets, second-hand clothes, and other items to the occupiers. Other areas included a medical center, a library, a kitchen, and an art/signs area where people painted signs and T-shirts. Slogans included the serious "Jail Corporate Criminals" to the humorous "I Bailed Out a Bank and All I Got Was a New Debit Card Charge."[66] The only electricity available was in an area called the media center. A portable generator provided power for computers used by volunteers who created updates, news, and reports for the Occupy website and other social media sites.

As a movement with no acknowledged leaders or centralized governing committee, Occupy Wall Street became an experiment in group democracy. A daily mass meeting called the General Assembly (GA) was open to all. Because police banned the use of bullhorns or amplified public address systems, the GA invented a novel means of communications called "mic check." A speaker would say a few words and pause. Those closest to the speaker loudly repeated the words in unison. Those behind them did same thing. The speaker would say a few more words, the chorus would repeat, and the statements radiated out to the back of the assembly. Listeners reacted in silence, using hand signals; four fingers up meant yea, or agreement; four fingers down meant boo, or negative; both hands rolling indicated that the crowd wished the speaker to finish talking. Reporter Hendrik Hertzberg witnessed a mic check and wrote, "There's something oddly moving about a crowd of smart-phone-addicted, computer-savvy people cooperating to create such an utterly low-tech, strikingly human, curiously tribal means of amplification—a literal loudspeaker."[67]

The Movement Grows

Whatever the means of communication, the movement was initially ignored by the mainstream media. That changed on September 24 when a high-tech tool, a cell phone, captured a video of three peaceful female protesters as they were pepper-sprayed by a New York City Police Department deputy inspector. The video of the women falling to the ground and screaming went viral on the Internet and drew international notice to the movement.

A week later, on October 1, the Occupy movement made headlines when around fifteen hundred protesters began a march across the Brooklyn Bridge. Police arrested around seven hundred people and hauled them away in buses. The arrest attracted some of the most powerful unions in New York to the Occupy movement. These unions, including transit workers, teamsters, teachers, and service employees, joined in an October 5 rally that brought fifteen thousand demonstrators to Wall Street.

By this time, the Occupy movement had spread to over a hundred cities throughout the United States, including Pittsburgh, Houston, Las Vegas, Seattle, and Washington, DC. On September 30 the Occupy Boston movement attracted at least ten thousand people. Many of the protesters set up an encampment in a park located in Boston's financial district. On October 10 about eight thousand people joined the Occupy Chicago movement to set up camp in a city park. The largest

Occupy Wall Street protesters make their views known during an October 2011 march in New York City. Economic inequality was the overriding theme of Occupy protests in cities all across the United States.

Occupy protests were in California, where demonstrations both large and small were held in over fifty cities.

On October 15, 2011, the Occupy movement inspired an international day of protest in 950 cities in eighty-two countries, including Spain, Canada, Germany, Israel, Brazil, Mexico, the Philippines, and Japan. While the protestors had a wide variety of grievances, depending on the locale, the overriding theme was economic inequality and austerity measures enacted by governments. Except for Rome, where police and protesters clashed, the demonstrations were largely peaceful.

On October 16 Obama expressed his support for the Occupy movement. In a statement the president said he was fighting to make certain that the "interests of 99 percent of Americans are well-represented"[68] by his administration.

Shutting Down the Camps

Although Obama and other politicians (mostly Democrats) initially aligned themselves with the Occupy movement, some cities experienced problems with the protesters. Most downtown districts, where the occupiers set up their tents, were not conducive to extended camping. Many places lacked public bathrooms, running water, daily trash collection, and other amenities. In San Francisco the city health department posted a notice warning protesters that growing piles of human waste and rotting garbage were attracting flies and creating unsanitary conditions that could lead to the spread of contagious diseases. Similar concerns prompted mayors in large cities, including Atlanta, Los Angeles, Philadelphia, New York, and Boston, to use riot police to clear the encampments.

In Oakland, California, attempts to remove approximately twenty-five hundred people encamped at Frank Ogawa Plaza in front of City Hall resulted in several weeks of discord. On October 25 police in riot gear cleared the encampment and arrested over one hundred people. That night, the occupiers retook the plaza while police attempted to repel them with tear gas. A former Marine and Iraq war veteran, Scott Olsen, was wounded in the melee, an event that made national news.

Declaration of the Occupation of New York City

On September 29, 2011, the General Assembly of the Occupy Wall Street movement issued a statement to express a wide range of grievances against banks and other corporations:

> We have peaceably assembled here, as is our right, to let these facts be known. . . .

> [Corporations] have taken bailouts from taxpayers with impunity, and continue to give Executives exorbitant bonuses.

> They have perpetuated inequality and discrimination in the workplace based on age, the color of one's skin, sex, gender identity and sexual orientation.

> They have poisoned the food supply through negligence, and undermined the farming system through monopolization. . . .

> They have continuously sought to strip employees of the right to negotiate for better pay and safer working conditions.

> They have held students hostage with tens of thousands of dollars of debt on education, which is itself a human right.

> They have consistently outsourced labor and used that outsourcing as leverage to cut workers' healthcare and pay.

> They have influenced the courts to achieve the same rights as people, with none of the culpability or responsibility. . . .

> They have sold our privacy as a commodity.

They have used the military and police force to prevent freedom of the press. . . .

They determine economic policy, despite the catastrophic failures their policies have produced and continue to produce.

They have donated large sums of money to politicians, who are responsible for regulating them. . . .

They purposefully keep people misinformed and fearful through their control of the media. . . .

They continue to create weapons of mass destruction in order to receive government contracts.

New York City General Assembly, "Declaration of the Occupation of New York City," September 29, 2011. www.nycga.net.

The situation continued for several more days, with police clearing the camp and protesters retaking it. On November 2, over ten thousand protesters gathered at the plaza. A small group set fires and smashed windows of local businesses. On November 21 Frank Ogawa Plaza was finally cleared by Oakland police.

As winter approached, most of the remaining Occupy camps folded. On September 17, 2012, the one-year anniversary of movement, demonstrations were held in several cities. However, the renewed actions attracted smaller crowds. While the Occupy movement had lost much of its momentum, the group's message continued to resonate. As journalist Stephen Zunes wrote on the anniversary: "Until last year, mainstream political discourse did not include nearly as much emphasis on such populist [mainstream] concerns as rising income inequality, tax policies that favor the rich, growing influence by large corporate interests in elections and the reckless deregulation of financial institutions that resulted in the 2008 crisis. It is hard to miss them now."[69]

Main Street Concerns

The Occupy movement helped shine a light on the economic concerns of average Americans. However, as banking expert Martha C. White wrote in 2012, "A year later, big, powerful banks remain big, powerful banks. Unemployment is still high, Americans' home equity and personal savings are depleted, and total student-loan debt tops a record $1 trillion."[70]

Despite these realities, the Occupy movement was credited with inspiring several moves by consumers, banks, and policy makers. One notable change took place after Bank of America imposed a $5 monthly fee on customers who used debit cards. This announcement came after Bank of America posted quarterly profits of $6.2 billion. As White writes, the bank "misjudged the fervor of antibank sentiment, some of it generated by all the attention paid to Occupy protesters. People . . . were outraged at their banks."[71] After thousands of customers called their banks in protest, Bank of America dropped the fee.

The move by Bank of America inspired a community action on November 5, 2011, called Bank Transfer Day. Protesters associated with the Occupy movement used social media websites to implore customers to transfer their savings and checking accounts from large banks to nonprofit credit unions. The action inspired eighty-six thousand people to move their money to credit unions. This was part of a trend that saw over $100 million transferred from big banks to credit unions in 2011.

The Occupy movement was also credited for prodding the government toward student loan relief. With millions of American college students unable to pay off their debts, Obama announced a plan to lower interest rates on student loans.

When asked about the impact of the Occupy movement, presidential adviser Stephanie Cutter stated, "The sentiments that lots of people who are out there as part of 'Occupy Wall Street' have—not just on Wall Street but on Main Streets across the country—those sentiments are shared by lots of Americans."[72]

A Lasting Impact

Whatever the gains, the recession continued to impact average citizens throughout the world years after the financial meltdown on Wall Street.

Although the US economy was in recovery, in 2012 over 40 percent of the new jobs created since the recession were minimum wage jobs, paying little more than eight dollars an hour. This left millions without benefits, pensions, and health insurance. And a study by the Bureau of Labor Statistics showed that about one-third of the 3 million workers displaced from their jobs from 2009 to 2011 saw their earnings drop 20 percent or more after finding new jobs.

The Great Depression lasted from the end of 1929 until the United States entered World War II in 1941. While the Great Recession technically lasted less than two years in the United States, the economy did not fully recover. And as the years passed, the impact of the recession continued to be felt in homes and workplaces throughout the world.

Source Notes

Introduction: The Defining Characteristics of the Great Recession

1. Hans-Werner Sinn, *Casino Capitalism*. Oxford: Oxford University Press, 2010, p. xiii.
2. Quoted in Marc Gongloff, "Financial Crisis Cost U.S. $12.8 Trillion or More: Study," *Huffington Post*, September 12, 2012. www.huffingtonpost .com.

Chapter One: What Conditions Led to the Great Recession?

3. Quoted in Jon Birger, "They Call Them Flippers," *CNN Money*, March 14, 2005. http://money.cnn.com.
4. Nomi Prins, *It Takes a Pillage: An Epic Tale of Power, Deceit, and Untold Trillions*. Hoboken, NJ: Wiley, 2009, p. 46.
5. Quoted in Gretchen Morgenson and Joshua Rosner, *Reckless Endangerment*. New York: Times Books/Macmillan, 2011, p. 95.
6. Quoted in U.S. Department of Housing and Urban Development, "Urban Policy Brief, Number 2," August 1995. www.huduser.org.
7. Quoted in Jo Becker, Sheryl Gay Stolberg, and Stephen Labaton, "Bush Drive for Home Ownership Fueled Housing Bubble," *New York Times*, December 21, 2008. www.nytimes.com.
8. Quoted in Nicholas D. Kristof, "A Banker Speaks, with Regret," *New York Times*, November 30, 2011. www.nytimes.com.
9. Kathleen Engel and Patricia A. McCoy, *The Subprime Virus*. New York: Oxford University Press, 2011, p. 36.
10. Quoted in Michael Lewis, *The Big Short: Inside the Doomsday Machine*. New York: W.W. Norton, 2010, p. 32.
11. Engel and McCoy, *The Subprime Virus*, pp. 4–5.
12. Quoted in Kristof, "A Banker Speaks, with Regret."
13. Matt Taibbi, *Griftopia*. New York: Spiegel & Grau, 2010, p. 134.
14. Quoted in Taibbi, *Griftopia*, p. 137.
15. Taibbi, *Griftopia*, pp. 135–36.
16. Taibbi, *Griftopia*, p. 144.

17. Carl Levin and Tom Coburn, *Wall Street and the Financial Crisis: Anatomy of a Financial Collapse*, US Senate Permanent Subcommittee on Investigations, April 13, 2011. www.hsga.senate.gov.

Chapter Two: Meltdown on Wall Street

18. Matthew Philips, "The Monster That Ate Wall Street," *Daily Beast*, September 26, 2008. www.thedailybeast.com.
19. Taibbie, *Griftopia*, p. 155.
20. Adam Davidson, "How AIG Fell Apart," *The Big Money, Slate* (blog), in Reuters, September 18, 2008. www.reuters.com.
21. Quoted in Paul Kiel, "Pointing the Finger at Greenspan," ProPublica, October 9, 2008. www.propublica.org.
22. Quoted in Peter S. Goodman, "Taking Hard New Look at a Greenspan Legacy," *New York Times*, October 8, 2008. www.nytimes.com.
23. Quoted in Robert O'Harrow Jr. and Brady Dennis, "Downgrades and Downfalls," *Washington Post*, December 31, 2008. www.washingtonpost .com.
24. Robert O'Harrow Jr. and Brady Dennis, "The Beautiful Machine," *Washington Post*, December 29, 2008. www.washingtonpost.com.
25. Quoted in Tom Petruno, "Mozilo Knew Hazardous Waste When He Saw It," *Money & Company* (blog), *Los Angeles Times*, June 4, 2009. http:// latimesblogs.latimes.com.
26. Quoted in Alistair Barr, "Moody's Downgrades 691 Mortgage-Backed Securities," *Wall Street Journal*, August 16, 2007. http://articles.market watch.com.
27. Levin and Coburn, *Wall Street and the Financial Crisis: Anatomy of a Financial Collapse*.
28. Quoted in Andrew Ross Sorkin, *Too Big to Fail*. New York: Viking, 2009, p. 369.
29. Henry M. Paulson Jr., *On the Brink*. New York: Business Plus, 2010, p. 236.
30. Quoted in Joe Nocera et al. "As Credit Crisis Spiraled, Alarm Led to Action," *New York Times*, October 1, 2008. www.nytimes.com.
31. Quoted in Engel and McCoy, *The Subprime Virus*, p. 121.

Chapter Three: Troubles on Main Street

32. George W. Bush, "President Bush's Speech to the Nation on the Economic Crisis," *New York Times*, September 24, 2008. www.nytimes.com.
33. Bush, "President Bush's Speech to the Nation on the Economic Crisis."
34. Quoted in Ben Rooney, "Bailout Foes Hold Day of Protests," CNN Money, September 24, 2008. http://money.cnn.com.

35. Quoted in Catherine Clifford, "Geithner: 'The Credit Crunch Is Not Over,'" CNN Money, November 19, 2009. http://money.cnn.com.

36. Stephanie Kelton, "Forget the Fiscal Cliff," *Los Angeles Times*, December 21, 2012, p. A35.

37. Quoted in Elizabeth Landau, "Unemployment Takes Tough Mental Toll," CNN, June 15, 2012. www.cnn.com.

38. Diane Hamilton, "How Unemployment Affects You (Even if You're Working)," Investopedia, November 11, 2009. www.investopedia.com.

39. Quoted in Chris Isidore, "Bush Announces Auto Rescue," CNN Money, December 19, 2008. http://money.cnn.com.

40. Peter Flaherty, "When Government Motors Fails (Again)," Real Clear Politics, February 5, 2011. www.realclearpolitics.com.

41. Quoted in Brian Montopoli, "Obama: We Don't Want to Run GM," CBS News, June 1, 2009. www.cbsnews.com.

42. Quoted in Michael Grabell, *Money Well Spent?* New York: PublicAffairs, 2012, p. 166.

43. Quoted in Steve Schifferes, "Foreclosure Wave Sweeps America," BBC News, November 5, 2007. http://news.bbc.co.uk.

44. Brent Larkin, "Plague of Abandoned Houses Requires a Unified Effort to Cure," *Cleveland (OH) Plain Dealer*, January 28, 2011. www.cleveland.com.

45. Quoted in Fox News, "Vacant Detroit Becomes Dumping Ground for the Dead," August 2, 2012. www.foxnews.com.

Chapter Four: A Global Recession

46. Michael Lewis, *Boomerang*. New York: W.W. Norton, 2011, pp. 1–2.

47. Paul Krugman, "The Icelandic Post-Crisis Miracle," *The Krugman Blogs*, *New York Times*, June 30, 2010. http://krugman.blogs.nytimes.com.

48. Robert Wade and Silla Sigurgeirsdóttir, "Lessons from Iceland," *New Left Review*, September/October 2010. http://newleftreview.org.

49. Wade and Sigurgeirsdóttir, "Lessons from Iceland."

50. Lewis, *Boomerang*, p. 16.

51. Quoted in Valur Gunnarsson, "For Richer, for Poorer: The Struggle to Survive After Banking Collapse," *Guardian* (Manchester, UK), December 21, 2008. www.guardian.co.uk.

52. Paul Krugman, "The Path Not Taken," *New York Times*, October 27, 2011. www.nytimes.com.

53. Quoted in Lewis, *Boomerang*, p. 50.

54. Sinn, *Casino Capitalism*, p. 245.

55. Quoted in Andy Dabilis, "Austerity, Depression, Crime Weigh Down Greeks," *Greek Reporter*, December 6, 2012. http://greece.greekreporter .com.

Chapter Five: What Was the Impact of the Great Recession?

56. Robert Hall, Martin Feldstein, et al., "Business Cycle Dating Committee, National Bureau of Economic Research," NBER, September 20, 2010. www.nber.org.

57. U.S. Senate Committee on Banking, Housing & Urban Affairs, "Brief Summary of the Dodd-Frank Wall Street Reform and Consumer Protection Act," July 10, 2010. http://banking.senate.gov.

58. CNBC, "Portfolio's Worst American CEOs of All Time," April 2009, p. 21. www.cnbc.com.

59. CNBC, "Portfolio's Worst American CEOs of All Time," p. 20.

60. Edward E. Lawler III, "Outrageous Executive Compensation: Corporate Boards, Not the Market, Are to Blame," *Forbes*, October 9, 2012. www .forbes.com.

61. Elizabeth Warren, "Tricks, Traps, and Accountability," *Huffington Post*, July 23, 2012. www.huffingtonpost.com.

62. Quoted in Edward Wyatt, "Dodd-Frank a Favorite Target for Republicans Laying Blame," *New York Times*, September 20, 2011. www.nytimes.com.

63. Quoted in Gary Rivlin, "The Billion-Dollar Bank Heist," *Daily Beast*, July 11, 2011. www.thedailybeast.com.

64. *Adbusters*, "Guys and Dolls," 2012. www.adbusters.org.

65. Occupy Wall Street, "We Are the 99 Percent," October 19, 2012. http:// wearethe99percent.tumblr.com.

66. Quoted in Hendrik Hertzberg, "A Walk in the Park," *New Yorker*, October 17, 2011. www.newyorker.com.

67. Hertzberg, "A Walk In the Park."

68. Quoted in Glenn Thrush, "W.H. with the '99 Percent'-ers," Politico 44, October 16, 2011. www.politico.com.

69. Stephen Zunes, "Occupy Fizzled, but Made 99% a Force," CNN, September 17, 2012. www.cnn.com.

70. Martha C. White, "Occupy Wall Street, One Year Later: Did It Make a Difference?," *Time*, September 17, 2012. http://business.time.com.

71. White, "Occupy Wall Street, One Year Later."

72. Quoted in Sam Stein, "White House, Pushing Richard Cordray's Nomination to CFPB, Cites Occupy Wall Street," *Huffington Post*, November 3, 2011. www.huffingtonpost.com.

Important People of The Great Recession

Brooksley Born: In 1999, as the head the Commodity Futures Trading Commission (CFTC), Born was one of the few government officials who called for the regulation of credit default swaps. After Congress passed a law expressly forbidding the CFTC from regulating swaps, Born resigned from her post.

George W. Bush: Bush was the forty-third president of the United States, serving from 2001 until 2009. During his second term in office, the housing bubble popped, the subprime mortgage meltdown ensued, and the United States entered the worst economic slowdown since the Great Depression. In his last months in office, Bush oversaw multibillion dollar bailouts of the financial, insurance, and auto industries.

Joseph Cassano: Cassano was the chief financial officer of American International Group's Financial Products (AIG FP) division from its founding in 1987 until he resigned in 2008. Under Cassano's leadership AIG FP sold hundreds of billions of dollars' worth of credit default swaps on subprime mortgages. In 2008 the federal government provided AIG with an $85 billion bailout to prevent a collapse of the world financial markets. Later rescue packages brought the total to $182 billion, making the AIG bailout the biggest in US history.

Bill Clinton: As the forty-second president of the United States, Clinton instituted the National Homeownership Strategy, a plan to increase home ownership in low-income neighborhoods. This led to a loosening of lending standards and the rapid growth of the subprime mortgage industry.

Richard Fuld: As the CEO of Lehman Brothers, Fuld was nicknamed the "Gorilla" on Wall Street for his competitive business practices. In the six years before Lehman's bankruptcy touched off a worldwide financial meltdown, Fuld earned over $500 million.

Timothy Geithner: An economist, Geithner was the president of the Federal Reserve in New York during the Wall Street financial crisis. He was among a small group of government officials who oversaw the sale of Bear Stearns, the bailout of AIG, and the bankruptcy of Lehman Brothers. In 2009 Geithner was confirmed as the seventy-fifth secretary of the treasury.

Alan Greenspan: As chairman of the Federal Reserve between 1987 and 2006, Greenspan was a strong proponent of unregulated markets. He often stated that he did not think that risky investment products like mortgage-backed securities and credit-default swaps could harm the economy. After the stock market meltdown in September 2008 Greenspan issued an apology.

Henry Paulson: Paulson was the chief executive officer of Goldman Sachs when George W. Bush named him secretary of the treasury in 2006. During the financial meltdown in September 2008, he conceived of the "Paulson Plan" to bail out financial firms on Wall Street with billions of taxpayer dollars.

Robert Rubin: Rubin was a board member of Goldman Sachs and director of Citigroup. As the seventieth secretary of the treasury under Bill Clinton, Rubin oversaw passage of the Financial Services Modernization Act which removed legal barriers between banks, brokerages, and insurance companies.

Elizabeth Warren: Warren was a Harvard Law School professor who specialized in bankruptcy law. In 2008 she was appointed to oversee the government bailout of the financial industry known as the Troubled Asset Relief Program (TARP). Warren was one of the leading advocates for the creation of the Consumer Financial Protection Bureau which was established in 2010. She was elected as a US Senator from Massachusetts in 2012 and assigned to the Senate Banking Committee in 2013.

For Further Research

Books

Karen Blumenthal, *Six Days in October*. New York: Atheneum, 2013.

Corona Brezina, *America's Recession: The Effects of the Economic Downturn*. New York: Rosen, 2011.

Dedria Bryfonski, ed., *The Banking Crisis*. Farmington Hills, MI: Gale/Cengage Learning, 2010.

Natalie Davis and Kelly Kagamas Tomkies, *Real Estate*. Farmington Hills, MI: Ferguson, 2011.

Kathy Furgang, *Understanding Economic Indicators: Predicting Future Trends in the Economy*. New York: Rosen, 2011.

David M. Haugen, *Reforming Wall Street*. Farmington Hills, MI: Gale/Cengage Learning, 2011.

Ronnie D. Lankford, ed., *What Is the Future of the US Economy?* Farmington Hills, MI: Gale/Cengage Learning, 2011.

Jason Porterfield, *How a Recession Affects You*. New York: Rosen, 2012.

Ronald A. Reis, *The Great Depression and the New Deal*. New York: Chelsea House, 2011.

Websites

Adbusters #Occupy (www.adbusters.org/campaigns/occupywallstreet). This website is hosted by the Canadian anticonsumerism group that initiated the Occupy Wall Street movement in mid-2011. The site features updates, livestreams from local protests, eyewitness accounts of demonstrations, and links to occupations in San Francisco, Chicago, Washington, DC, and elsewhere.

Global Financial Crisis (www.ft.com/indepth/global-financial-crisis). This site, hosted by the *Financial Times* of London, features an in-depth look at how the financial crisis has played out throughout the world from Wall Street to Moscow to Beijing.

Inside the Meltdown (www.pbs.org/wgbh/pages/frontline/meltdown). This site for the PBS *Frontline* episode features the original TV show *Inside the Meltdown* along with interviews, a timeline, and analysis concerning how the economy went bad, who could have stopped it, and the subsequent steps taken to fix it.

Money, Power & Wall Street (www.pbs.org/wgbh/pages/frontline /money-power-wall-street). Four episodes of *Frontline* that explore Wall Street culture, the lead-up to the Great Recession, and the reactions from President Obama and other government officials. The site features articles and discussions concerning the latest events on Wall Street and the recession.

The New York City General Assembly (www.nycga.net). This official website of the Occupy Wall Street movement is the work of several dozen groups working to maintain the momentum of the 2011 protests about the financial bailout, unemployment, and other social issues.

Unemployment Stories (http://gawker.com/hello-from-the-under-class). The media website Gawker runs this weekly series in which unemployed people describe their travails in often painful detail. Many have been searching for work since the earliest days of the recession, and their stories provide an inside look at the Great Recession beyond facts, figures, and statistics.

We Are the 99 Percent (http://wearethe99percent.tumblr.com). A website dedicated to the Occupy Wall Street movement that features hundreds of stories from average citizens who describe their unemployment, foreclosures, lack of health insurance, and other financial troubles aggravated by the recession.

Index

Picture Credits

About the Author

Stuart A. Kallen is the author of more than 250 nonfiction books for children and young adults. He has written on topics ranging from the theory of relativity to the history of rock and roll. In addition, Kallen has written award-winning children's videos and television scripts. In his spare time he is a singer/songwriter/guitarist in San Diego.